Victories
FROM THE
Battlefield

A Chaplain's Testimony

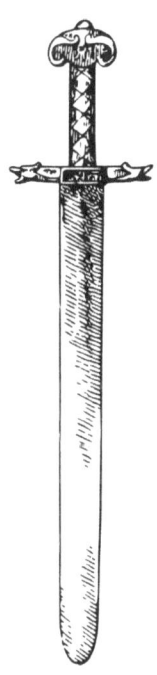

by

James W. Benton

Watersprings
PUBLISHING

Victories from the Battlefield
Published by Watersprings Publishing,
a division of Watersprings Media House, LLC.
P.O. Box 1284 Olive Branch, MS 38654
www.waterspringsmedia.com
Contact publisher for bulk orders and permission requests.

Scripture quotations are taken from the King James Version of the Holy Bible.

Printed in the United States of America.

ISBN-13: 979-8-9859594-1-3

Dedication

This book is dedicated to my family, especially my parents and Grandfather. My Mother, for being the first person to tell me about our beloved, Jesus Christ, sharing fascinating Bible stories with me, and taking me to church; my Dad, for protecting our home and making it a place where there was always plenty of laughter and peace; and my paternal Grandfather, for sitting me on his lap and reading the Bible to me, since I would visit with him three to four times a week after school. He always played the banjo and sang before lovingly giving me a banana, an apple, and some peanuts when it was time to leave. I think I became a Pastor because of what I saw in him, and he was a Pastor!

To the rest of my family: my children, brothers, sisters, nieces, nephews, great nieces, and nephews, along with cousins, for staying on my mind while I was answering God's call to the ministry. Hopefully, they will understand that the gospel starts with your own family and then goes out to the world.

Praises

Victories from the Battlefield: A Chaplain's Testimony

Victories from the Battlefield relates the dramatic daily conflicts between unseen "principalities and powers" that engage individual's lives and society in the real seen world. Raised "invisible," James experienced the effects of societal disadvantage and youthful mistakes. Yet, godly mentors inspired alternative life choices that guided him step by step to advance through education, practical experience, and professional ranks to become a respected correctional chaplain for troubled youth. Having learned visible truths from God's Word, Chaplain Benton skillfully applied Bible principles to his advantage defending the spiritual lives of youth threatened by the enemy's weapons of harmful crime, drugs, gangs and immorality that caused their loss of purpose, disrespect and despondency. Throughout his ministry, Chaplain Benton's vision expanded from the institution to encompass larger circles in the greater community. His positive influence of practical and spiritual programs changed contacts one life at a time for better and for God. Working in a world of religious pluralism as a Seventh-day Adventist chaplain, Chaplain Benton turned negative realities encountered into a positive victory of opportunities for the entire population (inmate and staff) of the correctional campus in which he ministered. This first-person story is a must-read manual that provides insight for youth leaders and chaplains on ministering to those youth often "invisible" by society in these challenging times.

Gary R. Councell, Chaplain, Pastor,
Retired Adventist Chaplaincy Director, M.DIV., MS

Praises

Victories from the Battlefield: A Chaplain's Testimony

If ever there is a book that gives chaplaincy the respect it deserves, it is this one. Filled with everyday examples from the successful career of someone who worked with incarcerated youth, *Victories from the Battlefield* details the strategies that Benton used to successfully navigate his roles as a chaplain/minister. His faith-based leadership acumen, anchored in daily prayer, provides a roadmap for others pursuing this career path and for anyone interested in a journey that wrestled the pangs of racism, confronted the crises of juvenile correctional systems, and battled spiritual warfare. It is a story of growth, strength, and warmth from someone "who always got [his] instructions from the Lord."

Dr. Valerie Lee, Author of *Sisterlocking Discoarse: Race, Gender, and the Twenty-First Century Academy*

For thou has girded me with strength unto the battle: thou hast subdued under me those that rose up against me.
- Psalm 18:39

Acknowledgements

To my beloved brother, Robert, who meant the world to me, my "big" brother who taught me about life and sports, always positive, motivating, and someone I could count on in all life journeys. I've been successful because of his wonderful love for me.

To my Mother-in-Law, who is like my biological mother, prayed earnestly and inspired me from the very first time we met.

To my lovely daughter, Angelique, who consented to be my "secretary" at just 5 years old, has consistently helped whenever asked and regularly types my sermons, cataloging and filing them on the computer.

To my devoted son, Tony, who has always loved and supported me in my journey. His presence at my college graduation affirmed his made-up mind and firm resolve to be in my corner.

Last but not least, to my dear, lovely wife Pat, who has always believed in me. Her encouragement has been reassuring while standing by my side, through thick and thin, financially, mentally, and spiritually. She also helped edit this book, for without her help, I would not have had the success I've had.

The words of the LORD are pure words...
- Psalm 12:6

Contents

Foreword

Chaplain James W. Benton, the author of Victories from the Battlefield: A Chaplain's Testimony is essential for those persons who are seriously considering the ministry of prison chaplaincy. I have personally worked alongside of Chaplain Benton, in my role as chemical dependency counselor and later as a psychologist assistant in the prison system for youth in Ohio. Following my retirement Chaplain Benton recommended, as well as became my mentor as a temporary chaplain in the adult system. My brief involvement in chaplaincy work (two years) was a success because of Chaplain Benton's influence, and my observation of his work as a chaplain. As a Christian, he is authentic, sensitive to the needs of others, often moving beyond the traditional role of a chaplain choosing to function as the pastor of the institution, serving both the inmates, their families, as well as, the institutional staff. He is well known for his prayers, advise, counseling and off-site support in times of crisis. His ecumenical approach endeared him to people of all religious faiths who found him accessible.

James Benton is astute in the urban youth culture, which served him well in the institution. The personal recollections of his career in Victories from the Battlefield: A Chaplain's Testimony, is a book that should be in the private library of every chaplain involved in prison ministry.

William-Amanze M. Pinckney, B.A., M.DIV., LICDC, BCPCC

From the rising of the sun unto the going down of the same the LORD's name is to be praised.
- Psalm 113:3

Introduction

I wrote this book to inspire hope and encouragement to any Chaplains, Pastors, or Ministers who are currently or who may be looking to choose this field for their careers. I worked 20 years in Corrections in the Department of Youth Services for the state of Ohio. You will read about real stories and situations that took place on a daily basis at times. By these stories you will see how God guided me and used me to bring peace and positive endings to all of the problems that would occur. Incarceration is not a pleasant place to wake up and be confronted with every morning. God would direct me after I had prayed about every situation that developed. God wanted to be seen, so that He could spread and show His love. God said, "They don't know me. Let them see me in you!"

God prepared me to be able to counsel and be an available source of help at any time. As a result, I was called upon repeatedly and believe you me, those times never failed. I learned that in many work institutions, wherever you are, there are always staff members who have not attended church, or have a spiritual person in their life. I would become their source of any spiritual connection and very often became their Pastor. I did house visitations, prayer, Bible studies, funerals, and hospital visits, just to name a few. Therefore, my ministry was quite full and extremely busy. Consequently, those individuals looking to pursue a career in this field could become more informed and gain additional insights from some of my experiences. I wrote these memoirs so I could also reflect back and see how God used me to be a blessing for others, because of how He saved and blessed me in my hour of need. Trust Him!

Early Year "Influences"

*"Come on, Bobby! Throw me the ball!" I said as I steadied myself at home plate. I gripped the bat tight, fingers closed in position, elbows extended, and ready to swing. I was serious. Hitting a long home run like my big brother and his friends was my goal. They were much older than me, but I had been practicing, and now was the time! I could do it. I **know** I could, but Bobby stopped pitching! "Come on, Bobby!" I said again, anxiously waiting. Then, he just dropped the ball. "I'm tired.", he said. "I'm going home." What? How could he do that! Not now. Ain't no quitting, neither! Uh-huh. I know that he had pitched to me twenty times or more already, but "this" would be the one! The **home** run!*

I grew up in Columbus, Ohio. My neighborhood was a friendly place. People cared about one another and shared what they had. No one acted snobbish, trying to be better than someone else or put others down. Parents looked out for **all** the children who lived there, **not** just their own. Many families were poor, but kids had fun growing up together, playing outside, and enjoying the fresh air and sunshine. People took pride in keeping up their properties and sat on their porches to pass the time. No one locked their doors, and everyone knew everyone else by name. Fortunately, I always got twenty-one!

My love and enjoyment for sports grew because of my older brother, Bobby, a "true" sports enthusiast. Being seven years older than me, I watched him play with his friends over and over again. Back then, they seemed so "big," and they were, to me, then.

Bobby and his boys played baseball, football, basketball, raced in the streets, and played many other games **until** the streetlights came on. Then, it was time to go. Every kid in the neighborhood knew that this "signal" meant to head for home and go in **or else**! No one **ever** wanted to explain to their parents why they hadn't gotten there on time.

Whenever I couldn't find my brother around the house, I knew exactly where he would be. Down at Renny's house, with the rest of his buddies! Renny had the **only** basketball hoop in his yard, and even though I was just seven, Bobby and his friends would let me play. These guys really taught me how to play basketball and treated me as an equal competitor. I got knocked down a lot, always had my shots blocked, and the ball taken from me. I learned, though, how to outmaneuver and better position myself to keep their attacks from happening all the time or from affecting my game because my teammates wanted to win! Everyone took the game very seriously, and so did I. I practiced daily, dribbling and shooting, and when I wasn't playing, I watched how they, my mentors, would fake, shoot, and block out for rebounds. Practicing paid off, and I got a lot better.

By the age of twelve, I could really shoot the ball well. Sometimes the" big" guys played a game called "21 the boot." Any number of guys could play since there wasn't a set number of participants to compete. One only had to be brave enough to play at all because **if** you didn't get to 21 and ended up being the last player, you faced serious consequences without mercy!

The game started at the foul line. Two points were given for each shot and an extra point for an additional lay-up. A player kept shooting until he missed. Then, he could take a chance and shoot another shot, **but** -- if he missed, his score would go to zero. The score of whoever was the last person out would be subtracted from 21. For example, if someone's score came to fifteen, it was subtracted from twenty-one, leaving him with only six points. The other players, then, in turn, got to "boot" him in the rear with their knee six times. Wow! I said you had to be brave and know how to shoot!

Fortunately, I always got twenty-one!

Thinking back, I have fond memories of my brother and his friends; Weyman, Bobby, Curtis, Leroy, and Forest playing baseball as well. They would hit the ball such a long way for home runs. I always wanted to hit like them during those times, but I wasn't strong enough yet. One day when my brother got tired of pitching to me, in frustration and disappointment, I threw the bat at him and hit him! He could have retaliated, but he didn't. Instead, Bobby continued working with me, and eventually, I succeeded. His friends continued to mentor me too. I looked up to my brother because he always showed me how to do something and then would encourage me during practice. **If** he told me I could do it, I believed him, and I **would** do it! Most importantly, though, his example taught me the value of what "true" sportsmanship was all about.

Thou shalt guide me with thy counsel...
-Psalm 73:24

Decisions & School Encounters

*"James Benton. Guard." I heard the announcer say. What? Was **that** all? The silence was deadening. No additional remarks telling about how well I had played! Nothing? I thought. After all the hustle and effort, I had put into being a team player! Not **only** playing my own position as Point Guard but also playing Center **and** Forward whenever the Coach asked me to help out another player in trouble! Wow! I had to know **all** the plays for these positions, and I did! Nothing? And now, at **this** momentous High School occasion...*

I attended Columbus Public Schools and went to Indianola Junior High. I played baseball and basketball there, but basketball held first place in my heart. I just loved shooting hoops! Bobby attended all of my home games and came to most of the away ones. He would even travel by city bus if necessary to see me play. His support meant everything to me.

Watching televised games, especially those of the NBA National Basketball Association, was especially thrilling and became one of my favorite pastimes. Most of my teenage friends and I had dreams and aspirations of going on to college and playing in the "pro" league. After graduating from Jr. High, I looked forward to making the Varsity Team my first year at North High School. I knew that I was good enough to make it, but, unfortunately, I had broken my leg and ankle sliding into second base during one of our Jr. High baseball games. Then, to make matters worse, once at North, I severely injured my ankle again when I came down on an opponent's foot during a regular gym class. With all of these sustained injuries, I decided to wait until my junior year to play basketball. The Coach was noticeably disappointed, and so was I since we both had been looking forward to working together.

Soon it was time for the school year to start again, and I knew that I was ready to play. During that summer, I worked very hard to strengthen my leg and ankle. Finally, I was ready and felt that this was my time! However, things changed. The Coach had accepted a new position to teach and coach somewhere else out of state! Something that I hadn't even thought about or considered as a possibility. Now, I was confronted and faced with working with someone new. Hopefully, just as good and as fair as the Coach who was leaving. But, I could tell from the very beginning that his replacement was different. He **did not** play the game using talent; **instead**, he saw "color."

I was crazy about my school and really looked forward to helping them win in the tournaments. Our team had never advanced to the playoffs each year; only one game and done! But now, teachers were being told that our school would have a chance because of me. In practice, I was outstanding. I worked hard every night and was the fastest on the team. Exhibiting the strong work ethic and Christian values taught to me by my parents and grandparents was crucial in molding me into the player I was becoming. I was a very quiet, respectful, Christian young man who did not curse. My family's consistent, positive example and influence paved the way and guided my footsteps and actions.

When the season started, the Coach didn't start me. Instead, he had me, for the most part, coming off the bench when we were losing at the **end** of a game. In the beginning, I reluctantly accepted the Coach's decisions, but after about the fourth game, I was puzzled by his strategies when we were losing with those he kept putting on the court. I couldn't figure out how these guys, who could not stop me in practice, were able to be **in** the game and I was **still** on the bench! I began to get frustrated but would never say anything about it. I just played harder and did what the Coach said.

I remember the Thanksgiving tournament when we were playing against South High, the previous year's State Champions. We had to beat them before facing the final contenders, Central. I did not start, as usual, and we were losing, as usual, at half-time. Then, I got word to go in and replace a teammate. We fought hard and came back and won! I got 25 points in that half of the game. Our focus now shifted to our final contenders, Central High, because if we won the next day against them, we would become the Tournament Champions!

The next night, however, I was right back on the bench. I got put in the game in the last quarter again when we were down by 27 points. I tried to tell the Coach about the opposing team's star player, Bobby Chandler, because I had played against him before, but the Coach refused to listen. As a result, Bobby scored 34 points against us. His team won the game **and** the Championship!

All that year, things never changed. I was considered the role model in school that teachers would point to as being a "good" student with "respectful" behavior. Yet, that year proved to be the first time I had really experienced and felt the detrimental effects of prejudice. I was the only Black person in my classes most of the time and sometimes got treated like I was invisible. Nothing was ever taught about African Americans, only slavery, and that was not explained truthfully. I began to realize and see things from a "new" perspective. It seemed like no matter how hard I tried and would be successful on the court and in the classroom, it really didn't make any difference. I was still invisible!

I recall how our Basketball Banquet was held at the State Fairgrounds in the Laushe Building at the end of the year. I heard rumors that I was **not** getting a "letter," an achievement award given for working hard all year and being a role model student. I shrugged it off as absurd. The time came, and the banquet was held. All the players were introduced, stating their positions and outstanding remarks about each one, such as how much hustle they had and their exceptional characters. Everyone received an award except when I was called, **only** my name was given and the position I played. **Nothing** else was said, and **no** letter was presented! I couldn't believe it! I was hurt so bad inside that I had to leave right then. My record was outstanding. I had never missed a practice, cursed, or complained. I gave 110% **every** game, even after coming off the bench at the end of a game when everyone knew I should have been starting. I was put in a game playing the Center, Point Guard, and Forward positions! I had to know every play in each position, and I did. After the "banquet" episode, though, I never was the same. I was deeply affected by people treating me as "less than" because of my color at that young age.

In my Senior year, I refused to go out for the team. Everyone said that this was "your" year, but I didn't have any more trust left in me. I did not want to be hurt again, so I **did not** play! Later on during the year, I was accused of influencing a few other players to boycott also, but this accusation was untrue. I never talked to anyone about not playing. I never made any trouble at all. I just never played any sports for the school ever again! Finally, with six weeks left before graduation and feeling that my dream of a career in sports had ended, I walked out of the school, never to return. I always had passing grades with a "B" average. I just quit caring because I felt that the coaches would never treat me with the same level of respect given to my teammates.

When I first arrived at North High that September, I was called into the Guidance Counselor's office. We briefly discussed my future goals. I remember commenting how I wanted to play in the NBA. The Counselor then asked what I would do if things didn't work out, and I told her that I wanted to be a Minister. How ironic! I never saw her again, and even with the bitter disappointment of a sports career ruined; God **still** had **His** plan for my life!

The following year, I came to games at the school because my younger brother wanted to follow after me. I would help him the same as our big brother had helped me. He loved sports just the same as we did. I was also able to mentor neighborhood youth and helped players on the team even though the Coach wouldn't ask me to come to the gym and play with them during the summer months. I was fortunate, however, to mentor a player named Dwight Lamar who lived in my same neighborhood. He talked to me after a home game in private telling me how he was experiencing similar unfair treatment by the Coach that I had gone through because of "color." He had been given an ultimatum - "Cut your Afro" or else! Dwight was presented with the dilemma of whether to relinquish his cultural heritage or compromise and give in to the Coach's demands.

However, Dwight's decision to stand up for himself and **not** cut his hair resonated with a greater impact than the Coach's threat! He took my advice and, for his senior year, transferred to East High School. He was successful there and got a scholarship to Southwestern Louisiana University, where he led the nation in scoring. Then, he graduated and made the NBA! Our neighborhood and East High School were very proud of him. His nickname was "Bo Pete."

3

Seeking GOD

"Are the Dead Really Dead?" I said, "Wow!" That's what I've been really wanting to know about."

Seven years later, I became the Head Custodian at Highland Elementary School. One evening as I was getting ready to leave, another employee informed me that while he was outside on break, two women came by and asked if they could use the school's piano. The church next door where they had been practicing was now under construction and unavailable. He told me that he had agreed for them to use the piano in the gym. I let him know that he should have cleared it with me first. However, since he had already given permission, be responsible and check on the ladies from time to time and make sure they got to their car safely when the practice was over.

Passing by the gym on my way out, I heard gospel songs being sung with such harmony that they captured my attention. The music was very calming, peaceful, and pretty. So I said to myself, "Go inside and see who's singing." The next thing I knew, I unintentionally had stayed for several hours listening. The songs were ministering to my soul. I'd been praying about getting my life straightened out. Asking God to let me know and understand the "whole" truth from His word was what I needed most. I wanted to go back to church, yet I longed for more of His word than I was getting from my child-hood Baptist upbringing to turn my life around. Situations in my life now had brought me to seriously search for truth as never before and I kept praying to God for it.

God answered my prayers. Little did I know then that He would use these same young ladies to share God's word and present more truth to me, who just happened to be Seventh-day Adventist Christians **and** Bible Workers! I was impressed with their musical abilities and went to tell them how much I appreciated their music. As I walked up to them, I happened to lean my arm on the piano and noticed an Amazing Facts pamphlet called "Are the Dead Really Dead?" I said, "Wow! That's what I've been really wanting to know about."

One of the women named Cheryl asked me if I would like to have Bible studies. I said, "Yes" immediately. She was shocked. At the time, I didn't know or realize why, but it's true discussing religion for many people is taboo. Some cling to their thoughts and logic, preconceived notions, or traditions about God and The Holy Bible. Whether right or wrong, they refuse to believe anything else. Others question God's existence. They tend to rationalize their self-sufficiency and have no time or place for God in their lives nor feel responsible for doing so. These individuals prefer to answer only to themselves, doing things "their **own** way" alone, agreeing to study God's word, seek truth, or get to know Him personally.

Since I stayed until they had finished practicing, Cheryl asked me if I would like to come to their concert at a Seventh-day Adventist Church in Delaware, Ohio. I said, "Yes," and bought five tickets, one for my mother, niece, two brothers, and myself. So we went on a cold, snowy Sunday evening. I drove. At first, we couldn't find the Church and were about to give up when we finally rode right in front of the Church's sign that said, "Victory Seventh-day Adventist Church." The concert was outstanding, and my family thought it was great. I remember telling them, "I **told** you they could really sing!" I even keep a partially taped recording of their concert to this day. The group was called "The Voices of Praise," with three female vocalists: Tonya, Deloris, and Cheryl.

It wasn't long before Deloris and Cheryl started giving me Bible studies each week. The lessons were so interesting that I began to tell my family about them, and soon my mother, Bobby, and niece joined us. After a while, Deloris, one of the Bible workers from the Allegheny West Conference of Seventh-day Adventists, was called to help Pastor Stephen Lewis do Bible work in Toledo. Being unable to continue conducting the studies herself, she contacted Carol Wright to replace her. Carol agreed. She, along with her husband, Pastor Henry Wright, and Cheryl, studied with our group even when I got my own place. They were glad to meet with us at any location, especially when they saw my enthusiasm, zeal, and burning desire to know more and more truth; for such excitement and eagerness to learn and study God's word seemed to be as if God, Himself, had lit a fuel of fire in me to keep searching.

As a result, I accepted all of the Biblical truths presented to me and became the first to get baptized in our study group on August 21, 1976. My baptism took place at the Ephesus Seventh-day Adventist Church, where Pastor Wright was the presiding Pastor. My mother, niece, and Bobby were there to see and support me. What an exciting, historical time! I was the last one out of thirteen to be baptized that day. Pastor Wright had purposely held me last to share my story of how I came to know the truth. My mother was thrilled.

Teach me thy way, O LORD; I will walk in thy truth: unite my heart to fear thy name.
-Psalm 86:11

4

Mama

"Son, I need to talk with you." "Uh-oh," I thought to myself. Usually, when Mama wanted to talk to any of us, it was for something we had done wrong. She had a way of telling you about it, softly and gently yet firm. And now, I wondered what "I" had done? Her room was "the" go-to place for these all-important talks. And now I found myself climbing the stairs, heading there, but for what? I couldn't think of anything I had done but -- maybe... As I came into the room, Mama was sitting by the window, looking out. Then, she turned and said, "I need to ask you a question, and I want you to answer me with the truth." I looked into her eyes and knew that she was extremely serious about what she would ask me. She said, ..."

The year after my baptism, 1977, October sixteenth, on a Sunday night, my dear mother was coming home from evening church services riding with one of her best friends, Mrs. Collins. They were broad sided by another car. My mother died a few hours later on the operating table. For me, that was the darkest, saddest, and most traumatic day **ever** in my life!

I was at work that night. Something seemed just not right, and for some reason, I couldn't quit thinking about my mother. I was so distracted that I left the job and went to the house.

Bobby was on the couch. I said, "Mama, isn't here yet?" He said, "No." I said, "She hasn't called?" He said, "No, not yet." We both felt like something was wrong. Then the phone rang. I picked it up, hoping that it was her calling, but it wasn't. It was a nurse from the hospital asking for "Jimmy," me! She said, "Your mother was in a bad car wreck. I don't think she's going to make it. I was told to call you." I said, "Thank you for calling." I was in total shock! I remember calmly turning around to tell Bobby but **not** share everything that the nurse had said, **only** that Mama and Mrs. Collins were in a car wreck.

As I drove up to the hospital entrance, my brother franticly started getting out of the car, hardly waiting for me to come to a complete stop. He bolted into the Emergency room, looking for her. While still sitting inside the car, I looked up to Heaven and said, "God, I **need** you now more than ever before." Then quickly headed inside. Mama had unfortunately passed away right before we got there.

My Aunt, my mother's only sister, lived several blocks from the hospital. We went over to tell her. She fainted and had to be put on the sofa. My brother and I couldn't get the support and strength we desperately sought from her because she herself was totally overwhelmed by this devastating news. It seemed as if satan had knocked all the air and life out of Bobby and me. Then, I recall being the one who had to tell our little brother, Pete. That was one of the hardest things I had to do. It knocked the breath out of him too. He almost fell over!

Everything seemed to come through me from that time on in spite of the fact that I was the eighth out of nine siblings. The next day, Mrs. Collins and Aunt Betty came over.

We talked sometimes or just sat close together silently in the dining room, and then my Aunt said, "Let's pray." I was looking for her or Mrs. Collins to pray because **they** were the elders who had been going to church for over forty years. Yet,

Aunt Betty asked me! I was a little surprised, but I prayed. They, in turn, were surprised too that I knew how to call on the Lord. Both of them were very grateful though for this and started counting on me to pray in every situation that came up after that.

My Mother's pastor came to the house the following day. I answered the door. He warmly gave his condolences, asked about the funeral arrangements, and said he would be back in touch. After that, every time the phone rang, it was for me. Looking back, I can see how God had strengthened me and was carrying me all at the same time. My dear, loving Mother was our family's Christian pillar and rock. The torch had now been given to me, and I even found myself being a source of comfort to some of my teenage nieces who would call me at night, fearful and unable to sleep. Answering every one of their calls with words of Scripture helped them and me.

We were never told by the authorities who was at fault or had received the traffic violation summons. Had Mrs. Collins incorrectly turned to make a left turn at a dual light signaling one to go with a **green** arrow, **or** had the young woman run a **red** light, hitting them directly where my mother was seated? To my family however, knowing who was right or wrong really did not matter now since it would not change anything. Mama had passed on.

I kept praying constantly for God's guidance, and about three days before the funeral, I called a family meeting between my five sisters and three brothers. When we were all gathered together, I offered a prayer for God to be with us and felt the Holy Spirit's presence there to comfort us because satan had seemingly been successful in viciously attacking our family. After talking a while about the funeral arrangements, I reminded everyone **not** to act out because our mother **would not** approve of any drinking, bad attitudes, or verbal attacks on others, as some of them had done in the past. Their actions were to **honor** our mother.

While in our mother's bedroom, we just began to talk. My oldest sister, Ella Mae, told of how Mama had called her to come over and talked with her right in this same room. She said that Mama spoke about how happy she was with her life and how God had blessed her to be a wife and mother of nine children and eleven grandchildren. Mama also told her how she had had a wonderful husband and married for thirty-three years before our father died on Christmas Day, 1968. She said she was at peace being a Christian.

Then another sister, Lois, then started talking and mentioned how Mama had asked her to come over and said almost the same things to her! The more we talked, the more we discovered that our mother probably had a premonition about herself because she had spoken to each of us personally, from the oldest child to the youngest. So we took turns sharing our last conversation with her in this same bedroom.

I vividly remember and never will forget when it was **my** turn. Mama called me and asked what time I was coming to the house because I would call and come by to see her every day. I came over, and she was upstairs. She told me that she wanted to talk to me. Whenever you had to go upstairs, it was behind closed doors. We would ask ourselves, "Okay, what did I do? I'm probably in trouble." But, I was usually the one taking the message to my sisters and brothers that Mama said she needed to talk to you. This time it was me! She was sitting by the window when I walked in. I said, "Hi, Mom." She said, "Hello." I said, "What did you want? Is everything all right?" She said, "Yes." I felt a little relieved. But after that, she said, "I need to ask you a question, and I want you to answer me with the truth." I looked into her eyes and knew that she was very serious about what she was going to ask me.

She said, "Did you ever think about going into the ministry?" I said, "What? "Has anyone been talking to you about me going to Oakwood College? Pastor Wright or any of the Bible workers?" She replied, "No." Then, I calmed down and thoughtfully considered her words before I answered. "If someone wanted me to go and do that, I would not do it. But, **if God called me**, I would do whatever **He** asked." My answer put a big, bright smile on her face, and she just said, "Okay. That's all I wanted to know." My mother never heard me preach for the Lord, but somehow, she knew the path God would lead me on, and it was enough.

Little did any of us know at that time, of course, what would happen later. While we all shared our stories, the Holy Spirit truly brought peace and joy during those dark days because death is **never** easy. The Bible calls it an enemy of mankind, for it brings pain, sorrow, misery, sleepless nights, headaches, and heartaches. When a death occurs, especially as an **unexpected** tragedy, it is even much, much worse. This devastating, targeted attack by evil is sabotage that purposely takes one's breath away!

Fear begins to capture your thoughts, and sometimes they wander out of control. You feel unprotected and completely vulnerable, knowing that the person you lost did **not** deserve to go like that, in a way you never, ever would have imagined. Then, you keep asking, "Why?" and you can't find answers or peace. The fear is really horrifying to the extent that some, who even seek professional help, never completely get over these tormenting feelings. Yet, trusting God and claiming His precious promises with time eases the pain and helps remove the fear of making living life doable again. As I look back, I am so glad that I knew Christ as my personal Saviour by then.

The Sabbath before my mother's car accident, Mama had told Deloris that she planned to surprise me by coming to

Church the next week and joining. Her decision had to have been the result of much prayer and being Spirit led because my mother had been a Baptist all of her life, even baptized as a child. I realized that for her to wholeheartedly consider becoming a Seventh-day Adventist and move her present membership meant continuing to follow God no matter where **He** led. Mama had been faithful in her walk with God. Faithful at Shiloh Baptist, before we moved up north from out east in 1960, and faithful still at Grace Baptist under the leadership of Pastor Mason, whom she was very close to. He even spoke of her unparalleled dedication and service, including being a Vacation Bible School Teacher, Choir member, and Cooking Assistant at her funeral.

I felt very happy to learn of my mother's intentions, yet her decision did not totally surprise me. On several occasions, Mama had commented that "all I have to do is change my cooking for dinnertime to be earlier and instead of on Saturday. Then the rest would be easy." Another time, we were talking in her bedroom, and while she started looking out the window right as the sun was setting one Friday evening, Mama noticed, "It's really peaceful and serene when this is happening. The birds go to their nests, and everything has a blessed atmosphere, just like you and the Pastor said in the studies."

When I was living at home, I also recall how my mother and Bobby kept witnessing changes they saw in me. I was not going out on Friday nights anymore but instead taking my baths early, drinking herbal tea, and sitting in the rocking chair reading Christian literature. Books such as The Desire of Ages, The Story of Redemption, and The Great Controversy, all by Ellen G. White captivated my attention. My brother told me that I looked so happy and peaceful, and that's what attracted him. Mama, too, watched me closely on Sabbath mornings while I checked my suits and tied my ties using the large mirror in her room. She told me that "I looked handsome." I could tell that she was pleased that I had the Lord in my life again and going to Church.

Before then, my world had been turned upside down! My son's mother had taken him, at four years old, and left for California, without my knowledge, to be with someone else. I was shocked, felt betrayed, hurt, and devastated. I loved my son **and** his mother, but now they were gone, just like that, and the "plans" I had had for us were **not** to be. How could this have happened? My son's mother and I had been together for six years. I was dedicated to her **and** her family. I always "thought" that we would get married just like her cousin, Vickie, and "Bulldog," my best friend. Everyone else seemed to know that her plans were completely different from mine. I began to change and did not fully realize how this void was negatively affecting me. I started staying up late and stopped eating right but continued to work very hard despite not having them.

My mother's house was in between my job and home. So, every day, I would stop by to see her and play basketball with my younger brother and nephews at the park until dark. That routine was helpful since it kept my problems off my mind for a while and was good exercise. Afterward, though, I would go home to an empty and lonely apartment. An apartment that I had worked hard to furnish, working overtime and staying determined so that I could afford two complete rooms of furniture. I had faithfully saved my money and laid these things away regardless of how others felt. Despite their doubts, I did pay for all of it and continued not giving up even though it was very hard not to think about my son and another man raising him.

My baby brother and nephews liked to come over, play cards, listen to music, and drink on the weekends. My nieces and their friends would call and come over too. My apartment was the "go-to" place, and I seemed to become very popular with them. Everyone wanted to hang out at my place. It was "the" place to be.

Everyone wanted to hang out at my place. It was "the" place to be.

One Saturday night, I decided to go out to this popular bar. The only person that I really knew there was a niece of mine. I noticed that the place was not that big, and I recall guys and women just standing and talking, leaning on the back wall. I sat at the bar and asked for a drink while the loud music and talking going on all at the same time caught my attention. Right afterward, the bartender said, "Last call for alcohol."

It was then that God spoke to my mind. He said, "Son, what are you doing? How much money have you spent this weekend? Look around." It seemed like everything had changed into slow motion to me. I looked into everyone's face, and God said, "They are not happy." I understood then what He was letting me know because I was not happy either. I didn't want to be there myself. I was looking for happiness in all the wrong places. Partying, staying up late, drinking, and smoking were things that I **never** wanted to be part of my life. So that night, I vowed to stop going to bars and clubs, and I didn't go any more.

I continued, however, to have the regular group come over on the weekends to play cards, listen to music, and drink. All that was keeping me from being lonely or having time to think about my son and his mother. I began drinking more and more without noticing how I was changing and what I was doing to my mind and body. I began smoking two packs of cigarettes a day and came to myself while talking on the phone one day. It was then that I finally realized what I was doing. I had one cigarette in hand and another one lit in an ashtray. I said to myself, "I'm getting worse. This has to stop!"

Then another Saturday night, I came home very late. As usual, I had stopped at my mother's house and played basketball until dark. I had hung out with my brother, nephew, and my best friend, and yes, we were drinking again! After leaving them, I remember going home and putting some hot dogs on the stove with the flame quite high to cook them faster. I went into the bedroom, kicked off my shoes, and decided to lay down for **just** a few minutes. I told myself I'd get up afterward and get the hot dogs.

However, I fell asleep. I don't know for how long, but I heard a voice in my mind say, "Wake up! Wake up!" I opened my eyes and immediately remembered the hot dogs! The house, by this time, was full of smoke. The pot and hot dogs had burnt up. After putting out the fire, I opened up all the windows and went onto the balcony for a few minutes to catch my breath. It was then that I realized how serious and frightening this situation was because nothing had ever happened to me like that before.

After the smoke had cleared, I sat on the couch. It was early Sunday morning. While I sat there, God began to talk to me. He said, "Son, you're going to die if you keep doing what you're doing. What has happened to you? You have wandered away from Me. You don't come to church anymore." Tears began to run down my face. My whole tee shirt seemed to be wet. I could not stop crying. He said, "I have always been here, and **you** left Me."

Everything was quiet. I could not hear anything outside or in the building **but** His still voice and kind spirit. I said I was sorry for my sinful ways and promised Him that I was coming back. After the Lord had finished with me and I settled down, I called my mother. She answered the phone, and I told her that I needed to talk to her and would be coming over. She said, "Okay." We talked, and I got straight to the point. I told her that I wanted to come back to the Lord and Church. She said, "Promise me one thing, that you won't play with God. Mean what you say." I said, "I won't, but I need more than what I've seen and heard at Church so far. I need the truth." Then, I felt I would be satisfied.

God answered my prayer.

5

GOD's Calling

*"I want you to speak for Me." I said, "me? I'm not worthy to speak, and I don't like being up in front of people." He said, "It's not you speaking but Me. The power is Me." I said, "Okay, Lord. If **You** give me something to say ..."*

The Bible Worker, Deloris, was single, and so was I. We became more than friends in 1976, and three years later were married in Durham, North Carolina, on the 21st of April. One summer evening, I remember her dad calling me on the phone. He was an Elder at our local Church, Emmanuel Temple. He asked me if I would preach for the Youth Week of Prayer in a couple of weeks. I was shocked that he asked me and petrified at the idea of **me** speaking! Right away, I thought, "No, Sir, I can't do it." When I told him that I had to pray about it first, though, he began to tell me that I was good with youth and that I could do it. I ended up listening to God, and I **did** speak! My very first sermon was on Jonah. Boy, I could really relate to the "running" part!

Later, my wife and I started a men's choral group called "Outreach for Christ" Male Chorus. I became the Children's Story Director and reorganized the Basketball Team, which became an "active" group once more since the previous team hadn't had anyone working with them consistently or committed enough to continue leading it. I was totally involved in helping the Church, because at the time, it was dying. My dedication to the Lord's work was recognized, and I was even voted Chaplain of the South Atlantic Youth Congress. Our local Church came back "alive" again, missing members returned, and new people began to join. Deloris and I also planned socials with adults and youth in mind. These activities were held on Saturday nights for fun, fellowship, and playing games. God was really blessing us.

In December of that same year, God called me to the Ministry. About two o'clock in the morning, I heard a voice in my mind say, "Wake up!" I opened my eyes and wondered why my wife didn't hear the voice. I was inspired to go downstairs, and I did. When I came into the living room, I felt the presence of the Holy Spirit. He did not make me afraid because He was peaceful, calm, and loving. But I was overwhelmed with awe, and I dropped to my knees and would not look up because I felt so very sinful. The voice in my mind said, "Don't be afraid. I want you to speak for Me." I said, "Me? I'm not worthy to speak, and I don't like being up in front of people." He said, "It's not you speaking, but Me. The power is Me." I said, "Okay, Lord. If **You** give me something to say, I **will** say it." My wife came in the room after He was gone. She looked at me and said, "God has called you to the Ministry, hasn't He?" I said, "Yes. How do you know that?" She said, "I can see it on your face."

I later became overjoyed with excitement. As time went by, days and weeks, you begin to wonder if you were really "called" or not. Right before Christmas, Deloris' friends, a very nice couple, Pastor Norman Snipes and his wife, were visiting the area and came over. They had heard that Deloris had gotten remarried. I asked Pastor Snipes about being called to the Ministry. He said that he would like us to come to Connecticut and visit them, and he would talk with me further. So,

Deloris and I went in June of 1980 during Camp meeting time. We stayed in their camper that weekend and early Sabbath morning, I got up and went outside. Getting some fresh air felt great because this was my first time sleeping in an RV.

Dr. E.E. Cleveland was walking that morning, and I joined him. We walked around meditating on nature together. I asked him if I could talk to him later about being "called." He said, "Yes." On Sunday, the very next day, Pastor Snipes took me into his study so that we could talk. It was clear that I was "called" by association and providence. He then called my wife in and counseled us on how to handle the calling. Pastor Snipes advised us to quit our jobs immediately, go to Huntsville, Alabama, and enroll in Oakwood College without delay. "The devil will not like your being 'called.' He is going to come in and wreck your household and marriage **if** you allow him to. Trust God and follow Him." he warned.

Several weeks later, my wife did not return home from work on time. I just thought that she was running a little late. Being somewhat tired, I decided to lay down and wait for her. I fell asleep. That night, Deloris finally called from her parents' home, but she wasn't talking like herself. She seemed confused and began mentioning moving and going into ministry. I told her that we needed to discuss the situation later and come home. Off and on, I heard her mother's voice in the background, sounding angry and totally against her daughter moving. Deloris didn't come home that night or the next night.

Two days later, I came home from work and went upstairs to take a nap. After a while, I woke up to this bumping sound I heard downstairs. I got up and went to the steps. From there, I saw a police officer pointing a gun directly at me. He quickly ordered me to put my hands over my head and come down slowly. I did. Three other officers were waiting in the front room. They had used a door ram to burst through the door. Then one of them threw me against the wall and started searching me. I tried to ask them what was going on. Out of the four officers, one was African American. They said, "We are taking you to jail." I said, "What for?" They didn't answer. So, I asked, "Can I at least make a phone call? I don't have any relatives in Durham." The Black officer gave me the phone. I called Bobby but, unfortunately, he wasn't home from work yet. No one answered.

I was immediately handcuffed and taken out the front door. My mother-in-law was standing to my right. She had been waiting for me to come out. It seemed like something was hidden in her hand, yet when I looked at her, she put her hand behind her back. "I hope they lock you up and keep you!" she said along with a few other choice words. I was in total shock! I didn't see my wife. Everything was going so fast, but I did see several of our neighbors outside and some kids playing from the area. I never said a word to anyone. However, after I was put into the Police car, I did ask the Black officer if I could bring my Bible. He got it and gave it to me.

I was then taken to Duke Hospital and placed in a small room with one large glass window. One of the officers was stationed outside to guard me. A hospital attendant came into the room with a straight jacket and laid it on the table. He quickly left. I sat in the chair and didn't move. I kept talking to God the whole time because I knew that I had not done anything wrong. The Holy Spirit said to me, "Just stay calm. Don't get loud or excited about whatever they do or say. Just listen." So, I began to read the Bible, one Psalm after another.

About a half hour later, a woman came in and introduced herself. She said that she was the Head Psychiatric Director and that I was in the hospital's mental ward. She began to tell me very clearly that I could be in serious trouble. I steadily looked into her eyes because she was looking into mine. The

Director then said that my mother-in-law insisted that I had been abusing her daughter physically, hitting her with a rubber hose so that it wouldn't leave any marks. She also accused me of mistreating Deloris every day.

The Director continued by telling me how that kind of behavior would not be taken lightly. She had tried to talk to my wife but was unable to do so. Apparently, Deloris was to upset to speak. Then she said, "Sir, I am only going to ask you this once. I can send you to Butler Mental Institution for six months." I knew that that was where Hinckley, the would-be assassin to President Ronald Reagan, was sent. "Did you abuse your wife?" I continued to look her in her eyes and said, "No, Ma'am. I love my wife, and I have never hit or abused her." She stared at me, looking into my eyes, and then said, "I believe you. I am **not** going to sign these papers."

The officer on guard duty seemed to be upset and left. I was relieved, confused, and shocked by what had happened to me. I just wanted some air. The officer refused to take me back home, so I walked. It took about two hours that night, but it helped me to think better because at least I wasn't handcuffed now. When I got to the apartment, I prayed for a long time, thanking God. My wife never came back home. I called her friends in Connecticut. Pastor Snipes though, never took my calls or called me. I felt lost but kept going to Church and continued working there even more. Deloris, however, quit coming to Church, but I still looked for her to come week after week.

After not hearing or talking to her for quite a few months, I went back to my hometown for several weeks. I needed to be with my family and feel their support. To keep me busy, I did projects around the house, one of which was fixing my brother's leaky roof. Then, I returned to Durham. Remembering Pastor Snipes' advice, I quit my job and intended for my wife and me to still go on to Oakwood College. Regrettably, I found that Deloris had moved everything out of our apartment. All of my personal things, such as sports gear, TVs, and furniture, that I had brought there from Columbus, were gone. I didn't know where she was or where she had moved to.

Because of this situation, I decided that going back home was best. I was able to get my old job with Columbus Public Schools and worked as a Custodian for three months. I really missed my wife though and wanted to be with her. I told my brother that I had to go back to Durham again. He did not want me to, but I went back in January 1981.

The same day I got there, I rode around town just thinking about her and what had happened. I remember driving over to the Research Triangle area where she used to work at IBM. Something said, "Turn right down this road." and I did.

Tall, impressive pine trees surrounded both sides of the road and eventually led to a new apartment complex that I had never seen. I turned into the parking lot and was amazed that my wife's car was there! I parked next to hers and rang the doorbell.

I saw the curtain move upstairs and her look down at me. I waited, thinking that she would come to the door, but she never did. My conscience told me to leave. As I was driving out, several police cars came speeding into the parking lot. God told me, "Wait. Don't move." So, I sat in the car watching and then a voice told me to go out the same way that the last police car had come in.

Even with all of this drama, I decided to stay and see if I could in some way reconcile with Deloris. Later, I got a room off Fayetteville Street. This was near the campus of the University of North Carolina Central. I wound up with a roommate who was a student there. He was a Godsend! I learned a lot from him about what it was like to be a college student because my plan was to go to college too. I felt fortunate to have someone like him to room with, someone who didn't smoke, drink, or curse, and we instantly got along very well. He was really a nice person who was genuinely concerned about me and my life. And even though I was much older, he respected what I was doing at Church.

I got hired by the Parks and Recreation Department and had a maintenance job at the UNC Chapel Hill location. Well-known NBA basketball players such as Sam Perkins, Michael Jordan, and James Worthy were all students back then playing college ball there. Occasionally, the maintenance crew and I would run into some of them at lunchtime in the snack bar. We even met the late, famous Coach Dean Smith, who allowed us to play "pick up" games in the gym as he watched. He noticed my playing ability and asked me if I had ever considered going to college and playing ball. I told him that at one time in my life playing ball had been my dream but now, at this age and the fact that God had called me to the ministry, playing ball was no longer an option. He smiled, shook my hand, and said that he understood. I felt ecstatic over meeting him and having had our candid conversation.

On rainy, inclement days, when our crew couldn't go out, I would put Christian tracts about salvation, worry, stress, and other topics in their lockers. They began to read and understand these truths. Somehow these guys found out that I was the one responsible for giving them the literature and, as a result, started coming to me for counseling and prayer. They noticed a marked difference in my character and how I didn't curse. One guy who came to me was a member of Shirley Caesar's Church. Soon afterward, I had the opportunity of meeting her personally in the mall. I was able to introduce myself once she gave her bodyguard the okay to let me pass, and then I told her about my working with one of her members. She thanked me, asked my name, and said she appreciated me helping him.

A couple of weeks later, I heard from my roommate that Rosa Parks was going to be a featured guest at the University, which was right around the corner from where we stayed! The event was to be on a Wednesday evening. I went to Prayer services on Wednesdays, but the program was scheduled for a later time, which meant that I would still be able to attend. Leaving Prayer Meeting that night, as I walked a couple of blocks towards the college, a black limo pulled up. To my surprise, the window rolled down, and there was Shirley Caesar waving at me! I waved back and then went on to the auditorium. Rosa Parks **really** was there! Afterward, I went up on stage and shook her hand.

During the six months that I stayed in Durham, I continued praying for my wife and her return to the Church and me. However, she never called or made any attempts to see me, although I attended all the area Adventist Churches, hoping to see her. Time went by, yet she still did not come back to Emmanuel Temple, her home Church. I never saw her.

Doors of Opportunity

*Oakwood! Oh, man. It's a dream! My roots. My parents are gone. Wife gone. thoughts all flooding my mind. "What am I doing here?" I'm **here**, Lord. I'm thirty-three! College! I thought I was going to Ohio State University when I was 17! Prejudice at North High School...fourteen years later... I always knew I could go. I knew that I could do this. I'm **here**, down at Oakwood, my walking stick in hand on the mountain, asking myself again, "What am I **doing** here?" and I **know** with certainty within myself, "It's where God called me."*

uring the spring of 1981, Dr. Calvin Rock, President of Oakwood College, was a Guest Speaker for the Emmanuel Temple Church. After speaking, he announced that if anyone wanted to talk to him about attending Oakwood College, then come downstairs right after service, and he would be glad to talk and meet with you. As I was going out the front door, my conscience said, "Go down and talk to him." I rationalized, "There's probably a long line to see him, and I won't get a chance to say anything." The voice that admonished me to speak with him became much stronger and now just said, "Go!" So I did.

I knocked on the door, and much to my surprise Dr. Rock was by himself! We began to talk, and he said, "Let's go outside and take a walk." He invited me to come to Oakwood and said that he would provide a campus tour plus my room and board for three days. I asked if my brother could come with me, and he said, "Sure." I gave Dr. Rock my Columbus address since I planned to move back sometime shortly after our meeting.

Living with my brother now, I anxiously waited to hear from him. July came, and I still had not received a call or heard anything. One day, however, as my brother and I were washing his car in the alleyway behind our former neighbors' garage, I noticed a large tan envelope in the bushes. It looked strange to be just lying there, so I picked it up, and to my surprise, it was from Dr. Rock! I could hardly believe that the envelope had been in the alley bushes and in such poor condition addressed to me. I hurried inside and opened the envelope. There enclosed was a letter with the words, "Greetings, James." It had the date that my brother and I were to arrive at the college and the scheduled time we were to see Dr. Rock. It also said to please call to confirm the appointment. The meeting was only two days away!

Bobby and I went. We were extremely impressed with Oakwood's campus. Dr. Rock himself was highly dignified, professional, and polite. We met in his office and got our meal tickets for three days. Afterward, he had us escorted to Edward's Hall, where we stayed. Right before our meeting ended, Dr. Rock asked me a very important question. We had discussed my marital situation privately before, and now he wanted to know what I would do if my wife didn't come back to me or join me there at Oakwood. I looked him in the eyes and said, "I am going to go on and finish because GOD called me." He smiled, and we shook hands.

My next step was to get my GED. It was late July now, and I contacted the proper officials to check out how to apply. I was informed of the requirements at the downtown educational office and met with the principal, who looked up my academic records. He could hardly believe that I had maintained a "B" average, went so far in school and **still** did not graduate! I told him my story. Then, he understood a little bit better how I was affected as a young person and my decision to leave before graduating.

Even though I had been away from school for about four-teen years, I felt that I could take the five required tests all at once. Of course, this was not allowed, but I was able to take three tests on the first day and two on the second. I passed them all! The Principal was truly happy and excited for me. I really knew now that everything was happening according to God's will, and continue to trust Him.

Doors quickly opened for me that summer. After finishing my application for Oakwood, I waited patiently to hear back from them. In the meantime, the Ohio Educational Department sent a letter along with my High School Equivalent Diploma congratulating me for passing! Then, the very next week, a letter arrived from BankOne verifying that my application for a guaranteed student loan had been accepted. However, the best news of all came the following week, when Oakwood College informed me that I **was** accepted and I started Fall Quarter in September 1981!

For me, going to Oakwood was a dream, a dream come true -- College! It wasn't an easy road but a very rewarding one. At the age of thirty-three, I entered Oakwood College as a Freshman. This was the very beginning of my Christian higher education learning experience. I loved the city of Huntsville, Alabama, and especially the people, all of my professors and students. God was in the beginning stages of giving me back everything I thought I had lost.

The first thing that God was doing was giving me peace of mind because I had been through a lot in the past and was still going through more. My parents were gone, my wife had left, and yet God put me where **He** wanted me to be; at a place where I could grow stronger spiritually, trusting in Him to lead and guide me each step of the way. The atmosphere, being down south, on campus, and feeling God's presence made all the difference. In every class, the professors would have a devotion and prayer before classes began. They worked **with** you, and their one-on-one assistance was priceless. These positive elements gave each student a sense of guidance, support, and courage.

I found myself meeting the challenges of college life with God's help. By continuing to put my faith and trust in God and His Word, doors of opportunity continued to open for me. I found that God provided jobs, housing, home-study courses, and transportation throughout my college years, from "borrowing" cars to even humbling me to "Get on the bus!" one quarter. This was something I **didn't** want to do and very hard to accept because I was used to having my **own** ride since high school. But then, in the midst of it all, God, with His uncanny sense of humor, made a way for me to take an Ohio State University graduate course as an undergraduate plus additional studies there for an entire year! I thought that I was going to OSU at seventeen; nevertheless, God **still** allowed me to attend seventeen years later despite all I faced back then! What a mighty God we serve!

I recall being in Dr. E.E. Cleveland's Public Evangelism class. He announced that he was going to conduct a tent effort in Columbus, Ohio the summer of 1982. I was excited to hear that it was going to be in my hometown. Later that evening, I went to his office and asked him if I could work with him as a Bible Worker. We talked about it, and he told me to come back the following week. So, I did. This continued until the seventh time, when he finally said, "Okay, you can help."

I had no experience working in a tent effort, but my wife had. Attending meetings with her on different occasions, I noticed what was done, and she knowingly shared the "why's" and "how's" with me. I was used to giving Bible studies and praying at people's houses but had never worked in a tent **or** been responsible for home visitations. Now, I would get my chance!

I was very confident and really wanted to be a part of the witnessing team, winning souls for the Kingdom. I had explained to Dr. Cleveland that I would be very useful to him because I knew the city well, the streets, neighborhoods, schools, and churches. He had the tent situated near the Allegheny West Conference Headquarters located at Broad and Ohio Streets. Dawn Lamb and I were chosen to be the official greeters and stationed at the front entrance. We met and greeted people nightly.

In addition, I was assigned to pass out flyers describing the meetings and topics. Bobby helped me blanket the whole area each week. We went from house to house around the tent and notified both neighborhood stores and businesses. Opening night was packed. Everyone who came out wanted to know, "Who is this Evangelist called E.E. Cleveland?" That night they found out!

Reporters, from one local newspaper, The Columbus Dispatch, witnessed firsthand Dr. Cleveland's effectiveness by God's power. They were so impressed that their Monday's edition featured an article on him entitled, "Dr. E.E. Cleveland Packs 'Em In." How true this was because "packing 'em in" described just how God kept individuals coming night after night for the weekday **and** weekend evening services!

What a thrilling and exciting time! The city's east side felt alive, and those who came seeking the Lord could hardly wait for worship to begin. Their anxious enthusiasm and joy were a testimony to the working of the Holy Spirit. Our team praised God for using us as we witnessed how lives were being changed.

During that whole campaign, I never heard from my estranged wife. However, one summer evening, I came in, and my brother sadly told me that I had a letter from the Durham, N.C. Court system. Several days went by before I opened it. It was my worst fear, divorce papers! I showed them to Dr. E.E. Cleveland. He reassured me that if I needed him to go to Court, he would testify on my behalf and be a character witness for me. Later, he told me that I had been set free and continue walking by faith, answering God's call.

In spite of my personal trials, I went on and became the number one Bible Worker for the campaign. God used me because I was positive, determined, and faithful to Him. We baptized one hundred and twenty-five people the first-time decisions were made to follow the Lord wholeheartedly. Then, a month later, we baptized another one hundred and twenty-five. These individuals formed the core membership of the "new" Central Seventh-day Adventist Church located today at Eighteenth and Oak Streets. Even after summer was over, the meetings never stopped. Souls were still coming to hear Dr. Cleveland, and arrangements were made for me to pick them up from all parts of the city, whether north, south, east, or west, in the Conference van.

I continued in spite of my wife's decision to get a divorce. Even though this situation and studying for all of my college classes were very difficult for me, I kept going. I didn't have my parents to talk to anymore, **but** I had my heavenly Father who continued to guide and strengthen me. By God's grace, I was able to finish school, just as I had promised Dr. Rock, and graduated in 1987 with a Bachelor of Theology degree. It was a privilege for me to become the very first one in my family to graduate from college.

7

Blessings

"Now is the moment", I thought. I had to do this. So, I took a deep breath and ..."

While going through my trials and troubles in Durham, N.C., I returned home in 1981 and experienced several reoccurring dreams about my home church, Ephesus. I was in my usual seat, a few rows from the back when a voice told me to look at the person several rows ahead of me. I did. Then the dream ended. The next night, the dream occurred again, the same way, with the voice directing me to look at this specific person. I said, "Okay," wondering, "Who is it?". The person turned around, and there was Pat, one of our members! I was surprised. Then the voice said, "Go see her."

I woke up. The dream was over, but it became more and more intense and urgently impressed upon my mind. I could not shake it. So eventually, I found myself telling Bobby. I was trying to make it go away, but it wouldn't. When I told him, he was excited and began telling me that "You know you have to do it if God told you to." I knew that, but I didn't want to. Pat and I were not close friends. I barely knew her but had seen her in Church. And now God wants me to go to see her after two and a half years! I didn't know if she was married, dating, or what.

I knew that I had to see her, **but** I was trying to do it by just calling her on the phone. However, it seemed as if I could never get her phone number. Believe me, I tried many ways but still to no avail. Every day my brother continued to encourage and prompt me to go. I finally prayed and got up enough nerve to do it. I knew that she drove a bright, yellow Toyota and was able to find out her address. Soon afterward, I went, yet all the while hoping that her car would **not** be in the parking lot. But it was! "Oh, boy," I said. "She's home." I got out, trying to guess which apartment was hers. I ended up going to an apartment **next** to hers and asked a guy there if he knew the young lady who drove the yellow Toyota. "Yes," he responded. "She lives right next door." "Okay, thanks."

"Now is the moment," I thought. I had to do this. So, I took a deep breath and rang the doorbell. At first, I made excuses hoping that she may not be home or maybe resting since it was about 5:00 p.m. But only after a few minutes, which seemed like forever to me, I heard a voice saying, "Who is it?" I said, "It's James." She opened the door, and I smiled, not knowing what to expect next. "I was just in the neighborhood, and I thought about you, so I stopped by." She invited me in, surprisingly. I remember her asking me, "Did I want something to drink?" I said, "Yes, water please."

During our conversation, Pat began telling me that she was engaged and going to get married the next year. Then it hit me why I was there! God wanted me to advise her to be careful and get the proper counseling before taking that all-important step. I mentioned my plans to go to college and how God had called me to the ministry.

She was happy for me and impressed that I accepted God's call. I stayed about forty-five minutes and then left.

It wasn't until I had completed my first year at college in 1982 that I saw her again. At that time, I was back in Columbus working with Dr. E.E. Cleveland as a Bible Worker for the Campus Cathedral tent effort. Sometimes she came out to the meetings and eventually invited my brother and me, among others, for Sabbath dinner. I was very happy to see her yet curious to know if she had gotten married. Later, she told me that things didn't work out. "Oh," I said and that I was sorry to hear that, but I also knew why God had used me to warn her to seek counseling first. Now, my eyes were opening, and I began to see how God had been leading and blessing me all at the same time.

I remember at the dinner how I had kinda tricked her into telling me her phone number. I told Pat that I had tried to call her and said the first part of her number, the only part I really knew. Right away, she chimed in and repeated the rest for me. I said, "Yes!" to myself. "That's it!" From then on, I started calling her almost every night. We had great conversations, became good friends, and enjoyed each other's company. We started dating and went to places like the Columbus Museum of Art because Pat loved art and shared her own original pieces with me. Going to Delaware Beach was another one of our go-to spots. Pat would pack a lunch, and we would swim, play Frisbee, discuss the Bible, and listen to gospel music there.

Church was a very special time for us too. Pat was one of the Sabbath School Teachers and went extra early each Saturday morning in order to attend the "Teachers" preview class before the regular class met. Her dedication was impressive to me.

Then, during the eleven o'clock service, we were excited sitting together and listening to the sermons. After that, church members started smiling and teasing us because they began seeing us together so much at Church, concerts, and other events. Sometimes we would hear them chanting, "Pat and James," "James and Pat." It was nice.

Pat and I dated for five years. We had grown closer over time and eventually in love. Through my struggles and trials, she became my support and was always there to encourage me when I was down or discouraged. Whenever I needed to vent or just wanted some company and not be alone, Pat listened. I knew that God had brought us together. I was a senior in college now. So, in February 1987, I came home from school one weekend, surprised her, and took her out on a "real" date for dinner. Afterward, we came back to her apartment that Sunday evening, and I asked her to marry me. She said, "Yes!"

Pat became **my** girl, **my** love, and **my** beautiful wife, whom I love dearly. We got married in New Jersey in July of that same year. What a wonderful time to be there with all of her family. The ceremony was just right; spiritual, exciting, and very joy-filled. We knew that God was present.

The following year, God blessed us with our lovely daughter on April 21. I was so thrilled and happy. What a glorious God we serve! I knew that the April 21, 1979 had been the date of my first marriage, **but now** instead of remembering hurt and pain, God gave me joy for the future with my new wife and daughter.

Our daughter, "Lee Lee," as we called her back then, was **definitely** Daddy's "little" girl. She wanted to go with me everywhere, and I took her whenever I could. Her mother would say, "Go ahead with your dad" smiling all the time. Sometimes, we went to the park on Sabbath to feed the geese and ducks or to the playground riding on the swings and walking around. Occasionally, we would go to the river and throw rocks, making them skip now and then across the water.

Bowling on Saturday nights was another one of our fun activities or enjoying "Lee Lee's" favorite pastime, **eating out**! However, to me, our **best** outing was going to see a basketball game. It didn't matter who was playing, but just having the opportunity to go was thrilling enough, whether watching NBA, college, or high school teams play.

These father and daughter moments were precious and still are. Our taking time out to be together and enjoying ourselves there meant a lot because she knew how much I loved her **and** sports, especially basketball. Sharing what was important to me with her was invaluable. Lastly, traveling with Pat and me in and out of the country was a blessing for us as well.

I LOVE the LORD, because he hath heard my voice and my supplications.
-Psalm 116:1

8

A Change of Direction - The "Newbie"

I was assigned to the Auburn House unit... responsible for "running" the show;...

n December of 1987, Elder J.O. Best and his wife, Nettie, Bobby, and I were riding together to do a Revelation Seminar at Central State College in Zenia, Ohio. The weather quickly took a turn for the worse that day with lots of snow and ice, but we were still determined to go. Unfortunately, we hadn't gotten very far from Elder Best's house when another car slid into us head-on. Everyone except Elder Best sustained some type of injury. My brother broke his nose, Nettie had several cuts and bruises, and I hurt my back.

Before starting the Seminar, I worked exclusively with Elder Best, helping him start new churches and support existing, small churches within the Allegheny West region. Elder Henry Wright was the Allegheny West Conference President at the time, and he agreed that we could conduct a Seminar program in Zenia. Due to my injury, however, I was unable to travel anywhere and was out of commission for about six months taking physical therapy. During that period, Elder Wright was called to another position at the General

Conference Headquarters in Washington, D.C. A new President was appointed, and our program was canceled.

After I finished physical therapy and felt somewhat better, my wife's friend told her about a posting where she worked that I might be interested in. The facility was called The Campus Chemical Dependency Treatment Center for Adolescents, and the position was for counseling youth. She thought that I would like it since I was already doing work with youth, families, and the community. I decided to inquire about the job and apply the same day I found out about it. When I got home, my wife told me that the Personnel Office had already called and said that the job was mine. I had never gotten a job that fast in my life! I accepted the position and became a Drug Counselor Assistant.

I really enjoyed working with the youth and meeting their families. It was rewarding seeing them finish their entire program. Some of my duties also included attending numerous training classes and workshops dealing with substance abuse, observing both Narcotics Anonymous (NA) and Alcoholic Anonymous (AA) meetings, and listening to many "leads"; the stories about a person's initial use with alcohol and drugs.

Unfortunately, after I had been working there for about a year, the company began to have financial difficulties. They had to close one of their facilities, and ours was picked to close. We had the option of going to Minneapolis to work, but no one wanted to relocate. All of the staff was laid off and began seeking employment elsewhere. My supervisor told me that I was an outstanding worker with youth and really had a "gift" relating to them. She recommended that I put in an application at the Department of Youth Services, which had about ten facilities in Ohio.

I applied at T.I.C.O., an acronym for the Training Institute for Corrections of Ohio, a youth correctional facility on the

Hilltop area of Columbus. Before leaving the Personnel Office, the Superintendent asked to see me. Now, that was very unusual. He interviewed me himself and even asked what I was interested in doing. I replied that I wanted to apply for the Chaplain's position. The Director explained that the job was usually never available since a Chaplain traditionally served until retirement. However, he had heard, that their Chaplain was considering retiring sometime in the near future. "Until that time comes, would you be interested in becoming a Correction Officer, called a Youth Leader, to get some experience until the Chaplain's position ever becomes available?" he said.

I got a call one week later, on March 5, 1990, my younger brother's birthday. I was fingerprinted, had my picture taken, and given my personal I.D. badge to wear at all times. During the first several days on the job, I was placed in the library and given the DYS Directives Manual to study, which was considered the Department's "bible," a must, to always know. As the years passed, I found this to be so very true. I was also given two eight-hour VHS tapes that reviewed verbal strategies and various scenarios involving youth. "Man Down" signals, an all available staff response to immediately help another Officer needing emergency assistance; procedures for riot control, fire drills, and tornado drills; and other pertinent information were included. Knowing how to use verbal strategies was very important because one needed these skills to prevent situations from easily escalating to physical hands-on altercations.

This required Library time allowed me to become better acquainted with the job's safety guidelines and precautions and provided a quiet atmosphere to learn countless rules and regulations. By being there, I was able to stay focused and concentrate completely undistracted by the youth population. I also began looking at various books and magazine titles on the shelves and was somewhat shocked to see so many inappropriate and unhealthy selections, in my opinion. This was a **State** Correctional Facility for the **youth** of Ohio; young men incarcerated for charges such as burglary, rape, armed robbery, drug dealing, and murder, to say the least, and yet I found reading material on weapons, sex, nudity, drugs, and more.

After finishing the videos, I next had to attend two weeks of unarmed self-defense training classes. All Staff, regardless of gender or job title, had to be included in these annual sessions. Some facilities even started requiring these classes to be held two to three times a year as time went on. The training was vitally necessary because eventually, one might have a situation occur that would call for quick thinking, on your feet, and using the proper verbal skills to keep youth behavior in check. Safety and security were always the first consideration to protect youth and, of course, oneself in case of being attacked.

The training was always held in the gym with the windows covered. Groups usually consisted of twelve to fifteen staff members in warm-up attire and tennis shoes. The trainers had been certified and were well-qualified to instruct us in these safety measures. Any restrictions or extenuating circumstances for non-participation were reviewed. Therefore, preexisting injuries had to be duly written about and signed on forms provided, or if totally unable to do the exercises, a signed doctor's excuse would be expected.

Instructions were clearly given before each session began. The majority of us really took the training to heart and enjoyed the classes because we knew that it was vital and extremely important to know and practice these techniques. The verbal skills, fight break-up, and escort strategies were the ones I would find myself using the most.

During these drills, staff participants had fun with one another as we partnered up and performed all of the various maneuvers on the floor mats. Afterward, everyone had to explain each technique and physically demonstrate the different ones when called out by the instructor. Then, at the end of the two weeks, we were evaluated on our ability to accurately replicate each move in front of the instructors before we passed.

Upon completing and passing the self-defense training, I was ready to interact with the youth population. Even though I was a "new" hire, I was placed on the first shift from 6 am to 2 pm. This was very unusual because all first shift workers had earned the right to select those times based on seniority and were highly sought after. My position, however, had become available due to one of the permanent staff members getting injured on the job and subsequently out on disability. I understood that working this shift would only be temporary, and I would probably be placed on second from 2 to 10 pm or third from 10 pm to 6 am eventually, yet I accepted. I needed the job.

I can remember being teased by the Superintendent. Sometimes he saw me clocking out when my shift was over and being randomly searched by Operations while going through the metal detectors. I had a large, black, plastic lunch box with a thermos inside at that time and the Superintendent would jokingly say that all I needed was a hard hat! He would laugh because to him I appeared to be coming from a construction site. Maybe that would not have been such a bad idea after seeing some of the things I would encounter.

Approximately 400 to 600 young men were incarcerated at that time, and I was assigned to the Auburn House unit. Initially, I didn't know anything about Auburn but soon found out that it had one of the worst reputations at the facility. What a challenge for me! I was "new" on the job, recently married with a grown son, Tony, and a two-year-old daughter, Angelique, plus I was a Seventh-day Adventist Christian.

In my first week, I was paired with two veteran Youth Leaders, one male, and one female, who had worked in their respective positions for about fourteen years each. Every unit had two assigned Youth Leaders. These two individuals taught me very well, and I mirrored their every move. For weeks, I'd listen to how they instructed groups and used their Walkie Talkies. I watched them do "count," where each youth would call out his place in line. I watched them schedule phone calls and patrol "med" lines, making sure that those who had medicine to take took it when the nurse came each day. I also watched and studied them as they did the school line and how they knew each youth's schedule and class times. They were experienced in using positive, verbal commands that were very effective, and I observed how these strategies allowed them to be in complete control. The Leaders could call the boys, line them up at the door, and have them quietly waiting so that when a Duty Officer came for them to join an existing line in the hall, they were ready.

Even when it was time to eat, these Youth Leaders would have their youth lined up and prepared to go when the call came because in the "joint," as they say, **nobody** wants to be late to eat! Otherwise, you may just not get the "cream of the crop" food items for the day. The youth knew that well. There was also one incentive plan to encourage them to take pride in themselves and work toward self-esteem based on an entire House working together. Each House was rated and awarded points for school attendance, room cleanliness, and no write-ups. Earning the most points for good behavior allowed the selected House to eat first and have their respective flag displayed for the whole month.

I learned that preplanning and punctuality with one's group were key because everything was programmed the same every day: count, breakfast, school, lunch, dinner, and recreation. If your group was late or unprepared for whatever reason, they would be put last, throwing off the schedule and messing up the day's activities for Operations and everyone else. Everything had to be timed. For example, silverware had to be counted and matched exactly - thirty forks and thirty spoons for thirty boys. If short, a recount was taken, and a search of each youth was done, **if** necessary. This delay would cause a "ripple" effect because time was wasted, and other activities were either pushed back or eliminated.

Youth Leaders had to be constantly aware of situations that could "set off" a youth, whether getting bad news from home, scuffling with someone in line, just being angry, or having a bad day. An Officer needed to be skilled enough to diffuse such anger, speak appropriately for various situations, and know how to 'handle' potentially aggressive young men. The Officer also had to use good judgment in properly controlling his group because narrow school hallways could become very dangerous. Rival gangs getting too close to one another or having to stop in a hallway was never a good thing, but if necessary, having total control was a must, **or** a riot could easily occur, especially with the dark, low lighting that we had. Since many of the youth had enemies, being on the alert while going to and from school and eating in the cafeteria was a necessity.

After finishing my "shadowing" weeks, I was now put to the test by being the Officer in charge of a Unit. One other Leader would assist me, but I was responsible for "running the show"; doing count when I arrived, med calls, school line, mail handout, phone calls, Cafeteria run, and the whole gamut. That first day was very exciting for me. I was not afraid.

I recall being eager and ready to let the youth know who I was and what I was all about. During the "shadowing," I listened intently and observed well. Now, I would be up front and personal. I was relaxed and very confident simply because my memory was good during those early years, and I was a man who believed in prayer. I knew God had called me to do this and that He was with me. Right from the start, I sat the youth down after I had counted and called it in. The boys were quick to hear and check me out to see what I was about.

Many of the youth wanted to try a "new" Youth Leader to see if the person was tough, sharp, or weak mentally. If the individual showed any signs of weakness, the boys knew that they would be able to manipulate that person into giving them whatever they wanted. Many of the eighteen- and nineteen-year-olds were big for their ages. Some weighed two hundred and twenty pounds easily, with heights ranging from 6'2" to 6'5". Several were 6'7" tall and even 6'8" on other units. Their physical appearances could be viewed as intimidating, but I looked them in the eyes and repeated the rules and regulations that they already knew to let them know that I knew them too! I told them a little about myself and what I expected from them because I was directing them toward manhood. My no-nonsense expectations included that their rooms be clean, with beds made so neat and tight that one could bounce a dime on them. No swearing and learning how to properly talk to adults, respecting them by saying, "Yes, Sir" and "Yes, Ma'am" was emphasized. They were trained to do just that.

My Unit was known to be one of the worst. We housed about fifty-two young men who had committed serious felonies. Some were gang members, "wanna bees", or just youth gone astray. Two to four of them were incarcerated for murder and would be "bound over" to adult prison after serving their juvenile sentences. Their misconduct led to fewer House privileges. As a result, recreational activities and supplies were limited, which made my Unit harder to maintain. One of the boys, for instance, had angrily broken the television set by throwing it against the wall. There was no ping pong table available either, just playing cards and sometimes chess. The Supervisor also had considered it too dangerous for them to have a pool table since an incident once occurred where a youth had badly beaten a Staff member using cue balls in a sock as a weapon.

There was, however, an active Grandparents program in place. Senior adults were permitted to interact with the Units every Tuesday evening. The youth loved it and were on their best behavior during those times, not wanting to miss out on seeing 'Grandma' or 'Grandpa.' These individuals were not biological Grandparents but volunteers desiring to mentor troubled youth and came from the greater Columbus metropolitan area. This program was outstanding but was later discontinued.

One observation that immediately stood out to me about my Unit was how these young men were used to playing "hands on" with other Youth Leaders, punching and wrestling at times. I did not operate that way. So, I set them down and let them know up front that I didn't "play" and was giving them fair warning. **Any** "hands" on me by them **would** be taken as a threat, and I **would** defend myself.

Since their actions and reputation preceded them, my youth were called last for breakfast, last for lunch, and last for dinner **every** day! Being physically aggressive to let others know how they felt about things that they were denied or wanted was what they were used to doing. This approach, however, was **not** effective. I asked them what exactly **they wanted** as a unit and advised them that the way they were going about everything was not the way to handle difficult situations. I let them know that "You have to work as a team. You guys get together, vote for a spokesperson, and get a secretary to write down your demands." Then, "I will meet with you tomorrow or later and go over your list to make sure that they are logical." They listened and began to trust me. I knew that I had to deliver on my promises, but first, I had to organize them before we could ever begin to be heard by the Administration.

The boys responded with a spokesperson, sergeant of arms, and a secretary. Their list was pretty good for the unit specifically and included a request for restored gym privileges since they had previously been banned for fighting. I set up a meeting with the Duty Officer after the youth had done their part in cleaning their rooms and unit floors and attaining better conduct in the hallways and at school. The Duty Officer listened to the spokesperson's demands on the unit's behalf and was very impressed with how they were working as a team for what they wanted. He said that **if** those on the unit continued their good behavior, he **would** get them a ping pong table.

To everyone's surprise, the youth **did** continue to do well and earned the ping pong table! The whole Institution could not believe the change in their behavior. The boys really started to see how respect is won; by doing what's right and respecting yourself and others. Soon after that, they also earned a color television for the Unit and moved from eating last at the cafeteria to eating first! They were not perfect, but they really grew together, learning how to become respectable young men. The big tests were always in the narrow hallways when other groups were passing by or vice versa. It was hard for them to take a lot of negative "trash" talking from the rival units, but they succeeded in ignoring the comments, to everyone's amazement.

Our unit really improved but we were still not permitted to enter the gymnasium. I came up with an excellent idea. I love sports, especially basketball, so one evening, I called the Duty Officer and asked him about us being able to play there. He thought about it for a while and then gave us one hour by ourselves. The youth were ecstatic and began to talk about how good they were, especially believing that they were better than me. We chose teams and had a great time. Of course, I took them "to school," or in other words, showed them that I was a much more advanced player than they were. I had "old school" moves that they had never seen.

I think they were in shock for a while. They really were happy that night. Having a chance to go back into the gym helped inspire them, and they wanted more privileges, and they earned them!

I began to teach them teamwork which was something they weren't used to on a basketball court. When I thought they were ready, I began to stir up a little competition by "trash" talking to the other Youth Leaders concerning their units. These Leaders really got a big laugh out of it. They thought my bragging was hilarious, thinking that they would beat us easily. My plan was to beat the "best" unit at the facility the **very** first time we played. Winning from such a team would give my youth the confidence they needed and would also strike fear throughout the Institution that "we" were a basketball force to be reckoned with.

The Duty Officer **did** let us play the "best" team in the facility because my youth had earned it. These two teams were the only ones allowed in the gym for that game. We beat them with teamwork and confidence running set plays. The other unit's team was shocked! My plan was working. We not only beat them, **but** we beat every other unit team in the entire Institution!

These young men really loved the praise and respect they got from staff now and were getting a "new" start. They began to believe in themselves and others and treated one another better and showed respect. The Staff, Teachers, and the Administration saw the difference. The Teachers were happy because the boys were, for the first time, present in their class-rooms and doing their assignments regularly. This had not happened before. Instead, they had stayed in their rooms and took "write-ups," the punishments for missing class, rather than attend.

All of these challenging events took place within the first six months of my Youth Leader duties, and even though ini-tially hired on a "temporary" basis, I became a "permanent" employee. The worker who I was covering for was unable to come back as scheduled. So, my "temporary" status was extended, and I continued filling his position until he could return.

Thinking back, I specifically remember a veteran coworker who had helped train me. She gave me a compliment one day by saying that I was a "hell" of a Youth Leader. I asked her what she meant by that. She replied that I was very different from anyone she knew in the Department or had ever worked with. "The youth respect you, listen to you and really love you! They do what you ask and listen to what you say. You never curse at them or have to raise your voice to get their atten-tion, **plus** look at what's happened to them in six months! You helped make that difference in them. I love working with you because you brought peace, and you're a joy to be around." I was genuinely surprised at what she said. I was never think-ing about myself but had been praying all along for the boys, seeking ways to help them grow into respectable young men with a future to look forward to.

9

Moving On To Buckeye & Buckeye Challenges

...the time had come to leave.

Soon afterward, I decided to move on, striving to reach higher goals. I was always checking job postings listed at our building's front entrance. To my surprise, Buckeye Youth Correctional Institution, a facility right next door, had two openings for Substance Abuse Counselors. I applied, and after only one interview, I was hired. It was then that I told the Administration at T.I.C.O. how much I appreciated everything they had done for me, but the time had come to leave.

Many of the African American Youth Leaders were shocked that I came and was about to leave so quickly. For you see, many of them had qualified for positions yet gave up trying to apply for specific jobs because they believed that they would **never** actually get one. What they were saying by their actions did have some validity because, unfortunately, most of them were **not** getting promoted **even** when absolutely qualified and should have been selected. I knew, however, that I was not one who easily gave up on anything. I had **already** applied for the listed Substance Abuse postings at T.I.C.O. before and had given them ample opportunity to hire me first for these programs. I was interviewed twice **yet** never chosen!

As a result, I went to Buckeye Youth Center and became one of **their** Substance Abuse Counselors. The atmosphere was quite different here. The building seemed newer, and the Staff appeared to be more relaxed, playful, and not as tense. After about three months, I unexpectedly received a call from T.I.C.O. asking me if I would come back and run **their** Substance Abuse program! I felt though that I had already given them several chances to select me, "but someone did not get the memo," and therefore decided that it would be best to remain where I was. I really enjoyed working at Buckeye and knew that God had led me there for a special purpose.

Buckeye did not have any successful Substance Abuse Teachers or Counselors to take over and run the department for their school. This was a real problem. They genuinely needed help, and two other individuals, one male and one female were hired for the position at the same time that I was. We became very close friends while putting together the most engaging and interactive programs for the Center. Mr. D and I held the morning classes, and Miss B. held the evening classes. We made learning about drug abuse fun. Other instructors had failed to spark any interest from the youth, and in turn, the youth refused to come to their classes.

In the beginning, designing exciting and attention-grabbing lessons was challenging. However, once we started working together and talking to different teachers, we were able to come up with various ideas that got us started on the right track. We all combined our strengths and used the treatment plans, movies, and tests in a structured and uniform manner. Others began to notice the continuity and effectiveness of our strategies. We kept good attendance records and therefore knew who was not showing up. Soon the school office started seeing the change in attendance and a "new" excitement among the youth.

We made learning fun. For example, one method that I used to generate and keep interest in class was by using an old television game called "Password" to teach drug terminology. Game rules were kept simple and reviewed. Youth could not use their hands in any way as they sat across from one another at tables, and only one-word clues could be given, not sentences, to get the person directly facing them to say the winning word. "Password" motivated them to concentrate and use their brains more constructively, something they were not accustomed to doing. The boys loved this game and never grew tired of it. This was a win-win situation because they learned the drug terms while at the same time having fun.

Another effective strategy that I used was employing skits and role playing. For example, I acted the part of a successful business owner conducting interviews for filling company vacancies. My purpose for this activity was to emphasize the importance of getting a quality education and knowing "how" to look and be professional, especially when applying for employment. We practiced the proper way of filling out applications, reviewed appropriate and inappropriate attire, discussed body language, acceptable speech, and eye contact, and how being adequately prepared and knowledgeable about a job's specifics was beneficial.

The boys had the chance to participate, and role play different characters and scenarios for certain businesses like McDonalds. I would then go to the board and, using this business as an example, write "Working at McDonald's" on one side and "Drug Dealing" on the other. Next, I would list five positive reasons to consider for sticking with McDonald's, such as: 1. Paycheck, 2. Job Skills, 3. Self-Esteem, 4. Respect, and 5. Future Life. I would speak at length on the impact of each of these areas as well as mentioned that their mindset should be to "Go in there with the goal of one day **'owning'** the place." Also, I would encourage them to "learn how to do all of the jobs necessary to operate the business from mopping floors, to cleaning tables, to flipping burgers, to running the cash register."

After that, I would present five negative reasons to consider for eliminating Drug Dealing from their life ambitions such as 1. Dangerous, 2. Breaking the Law, 3. Shoot-Outs on the Block, 4. Paranoia, and 5. No Future - Prison. I would talk at length about each of these factors too. On the street, they knew that you don't make any money until you "flip" the money, which means that you receive a small percentage of the total gross funds. (Maybe $10/$100.) When they saw the facts listed on the board and rationale for each side, it made more sense to choose McDonald's. I gave them other business possibilities as well to expand their thinking. One idea for them to consider was shoveling snow for homeowners during the winter months to establish a set clientele and then offer grass cutting services, including yard maintenance in the summer months. This business plan would enable them to be employed year-round and work for themselves or learn under a reputable company already established until they are able to venture out on their own.

Our Substance Abuse program's movie component used movie presentations that were strictly substance abuse related; true stories about those who overcame after hitting rock bottom in life. In conjunction with these movies, I ran the N.A., Narcotics Anonymous, and A.A., Alcoholics Anonymous, groups every Thursday night. I invited people from the community to come and give what is called a "lead," meaning that they would tell the group how they got started using drugs and or alcohol and what it did to their lives. These sessions were very dynamic and powerful. The young men honestly looked forward to coming each week as much as I looked forward to having new guests as well.

At the end of the quarter, I would have finals and graduation parties for my classes. It was great getting the boys started on the right road and watching their self-esteem develop. Teachers, Unit Managers, Social Workers, and others saw these positive changes occur. They were proud to have our team on board with them.

Soon the youth spread the word about my classes, and they filled quickly. We had to sign youth up for the whole year with a waiting list, and some who had even graduated were trying to get **back** in! I guess this was when T.I.C.O. wanted me back, but I turned them down because I appreciated Buckeye for giving me the opportunity to show what I could do to help make a positive difference.

In 1991, the State of Ohio Governor's Office had a recognition program entitled "The State Employee Suggestion Award Program." It was designed for all State workers to submit any ideas and suggestions to help make improvements at their respective workplaces. I applied with my concerns over the "unhealthy" books laden with sex, violence, and crime being readily available in the institution libraries. Videos, with the same content and glorifying the same negative elements as the books; were also easily being brought in and shown on Units.

I wrote about the objectionable effects of both the books and the videos, emphasizing their undesirable influence on youth who were already locked up for breaking the laws that these materials promoted. As part of the submission, I had to write a solution to the problem. I did so by suggesting a policy be in place requiring a checklist of appropriate books, magazines, and articles that would be permitted. My comments regarding videos addressed having Security Officers do a better job at checking Staff for contraband items. In addition, each institution would keep a checklist of pre-approved videos and mandate that **only** those having **prior** approval by a chosen committee could be shown. These recommendations were accepted as policy and endorsed for **all** the Department of Youth Services' facilities! I received an award from Governor Voinovich on April 20, 1992, for helping to alleviate this situation. [see Photo]

One day while I was enjoying teaching my classes, I got a call to come in from the Central Office downtown. I was informed to notify the other two Counselors that the Department's Drug Unit would be coming unannounced sometime during the next week to conduct drug searches and would be bringing specially trained dogs with them. They had received several calls about drugs possibly coming into the facility and wanted to check themselves. The Search Team came and surprised the Youth Leaders in charge of each House in a day or two. A thorough check was made on all Units, looking under beds, mattresses, ceiling tiles, and wherever else they could think of including checking parked cars for drugs and contraband.

These employees were very upset because everything was disrupted, and as I recall, a few of them got called in for questioning. Not very long after that, my Volkswagen got "keyed" from the headlight to the taillight. I was upset about this and told the Administration, but nothing was done. I honestly felt that a "guilty" worker thought that I was responsible for the search since I was one of the "new" Counselors there.

The Substance Abuse Department's programming approach steadily improved the Institution with the Drug Awareness classes provided and educational sessions planned for the young men. After about a year, the entire Institution continued to see marked improvements in youth behavior and attendance. We stayed busy, yet from the time that I arrived, there were rumors always going around saying that our facility, Buckeye Youth Center, was going to move **out** of Columbus. We heard this year after year, **but** in 1993, the rumor became a reality!

While at Buckeye, I attended Church with the youth whenever I was scheduled to work on a Sunday. I made sure that I met Chaplain Mabian Sanners and always went to his programs and Church services whenever possible. We became close friends soon afterward. He then began introducing me to his volunteers, both individuals and groups, who did ministry at the facility. These people included Sister M. of the Sacred Heart, the men's group from World Harvest, Grandparents from the Columbus metropolitan area, and Guest Pastors who came in for special Church events. Then Chaplain Mabian Sanners started inviting me to go off grounds with him to his Ohio State Chaplain Association and Ministerial Alliance Pastor's meetings in Columbus and later Circleville. The majority of the Clergy were friendly, and I began to learn a lot from being at these sessions. Chaplain Mabian Sanners also made sure to invite me to be with him at his volunteer banquets, where I met more of his work team.

I will go in the strength of the Lord GOD...
-Psalm 71:16

More Work to Do

God worked in a mighty way in opening doors for me while working with these young women.

Passing by the bulletin board at the job one day, I read about a posting for the Freedom Center. This was a Substance Abuse Center for teen girls also under the Department of Youth Services. They were in need of a part-time contract Chaplain, so I applied. Normally, you couldn't be a full-time employee and contract at the same time, but I got the job because of my character references, experience, and education.

The girls at the Center had drug problems and were required to have treatment before being released. My job was to provide the Church services, spiritual counseling, prayer, and Bible Studies, totaling twelve to fifteen hours per week. I had volunteers come in from various local area churches. They conducted the services at times and even held workshops. Some of these workshops included: motherhood, personal hygiene, proper use of make-up, dating, and songwriting. Several professional singers came as well and gave concerts for the girls along with inspiring, motivational talks to boost and build up their self-esteem.

Saturday nights were extra-special times. I taught them how they could have a lot of fun without drinking or using any drugs by playing Church games, like "Silly," "What's That You Said About Me?" (a version of the old gossip game), and "In the River, On the Bank." The girls had a ball, laughing hysterically, and didn't even want to stop when it was time for me to leave. [see Appendix]

On Sunday mornings, there was usually one hundred percent attendance for the Church worship services. This was fantastic! Afterward, a staff employee we called "Mom" would cook a big dinner for all the girls. She and other volunteers were instrumental in teaching them how to knit. They made beautiful blankets for the homeless and the YMCA. Then, once a quarter, I helped the teens hold a car wash to raise the expense money needed to buy the yarn for this community project. The entire Staff encouraged each of them to be involved in this worthy endeavor for the benefit of others.

Now with their newly acquired skill, the girls asked me if I wanted a sports blanket since they knew that I liked the Cleveland Browns, football team. I appreciated their thoughtfulness and agreed to let them do one for me. I bought the orange, brown, and white yarn for it, and after church one Sunday, they surprised me with a striped blanket that represented the team well. All of them had taken turns knitting it because I was so tall. I still have the blanket in my sports room today and display it gratefully when I'm watching the Browns play.

God worked in a mighty way in opening doors for me while working with these young women. For example, I can remember getting permission to take those who were Catholic next door for Mass. Another time, I obtained permission from the Superintendent so that girls who requested to be baptized could be after receiving their parent's signed consent.

Pastor Latta of the Hilltop Bible Way Church, on the west side of Columbus, was very gracious and allowed me to use his Church for the baptisms. Then, I was allowed to take the girls on tours of important places in the city. We rode downtown, not far away.

I showed them the Statehouse, City Hall, and historical movie theaters like the Southern and the Palace. I gave them pertinent background information on how things were "back in the day," my day, and how everyone would go to these venues to see top entertainers and movie stars on Saturday nights like Etta James, Ike and Tina Turner, James Brown, and Sammy Davis, Jr.

Our tour list also included The Ohio State University. I had often talked to these young women about the importance of education and encouraged them to finish school and go on to college or even receive some type of vocational training. I urged them that **if** it were possible, in any way, **go after** their goals and dreams! I showed them the Horseshoe Stadium. They saw cheerleaders practicing on campus and the joyful atmosphere that surrounded the grounds. They especially liked, of course, seeing all the boys who were walking and talking to girls and playing basketball. We had a great time there, walking around, talking, and sitting on the lawn watching students' dogs catch Frisbees.

On a different occasion, the girls were allowed to go to Delaware Metro Park Beach because of their good behavior and the extremely hot weather we had experienced all that week. It was decided at the facility that this would be a great idea to take them.

The girls really enjoyed running, laughing, and being out in the fresh air. They walked in the wet sand along the shore and made sandcastles. I did not allow them to swim, however. The last outing, we took was to my own home Church,

Ephesus Seventh-day Adventist Church. The girls wanted to visit and see what church life was like for youth their own age and from a Christian youth's perspective. I brought seven young women to the A.Y.S. Adventist Youth Society, meeting that was held in the late afternoon on Saturday, the Sabbath. This meeting turned out to be a good experience for them. The Freedom Center girls met families, as well as young people their own age and were able to converse and see what life was like in their world, the "world" of being a Christian young person. The girls said that they had genuinely enjoyed the fellowship.

The New Move - Cir Bound

...signed, sealed, and ready to go.

Finally, word came from Central Office that moving out of Columbus to a "new" facility was no longer a rumor. Buckeye employees were told to pack up all of our files and personal things; boxed, signed, sealed, and ready to go. We officially moved to Cir in 1993. One department was moved at a time, in shifts, until each division arrived successfully.

That same summer, the grand opening of the Cir Juvenile Youth Facility was held. Dignitaries, including the town's Mayor, Central Office Director, chief staff, T.I.C.O.'s Honor Guard, and several top officials from the Governor's Office, were there. This was a very impressive opening, complete with the ribbon cutting ceremony outside and Cir's Mayor welcoming the "new" Juvenile Correctional Staff to their community. Indeed a "big" day for the Department of Youth Services as well because of its significant undertaking in building this fourteen-million-dollar facility outside of Columbus, the very first of three!

It was not long after we officially started that things got bumpy and rough for employees. The Superintendent that originally came with us from Buckeye **never** really started at Cir! He just disappeared, even though this was his hometown. We soon got another Superintendent, but our initial

Superintendent's leaving, so unexpected and puzzling, seemed to start a trend of not having the Superintendents stay for very long. I think we had about nineteen different ones during my tenure there. Something was not right! My mother always told me, "What doesn't come out in the wash will sometimes come out in the rinse." Time will tell.

Problems began occurring everywhere! Some were to be expected with a brand-new facility, **but** many were totally unnecessary. Once, several Social Workers and Substance Abuse Counselors had to stay in my housing unit with the youth because our own offices were flooded! Three to four inches of water on the floors, already?

And then, to make matters worse, since we were not issued keys to any of the unit security doors or "flooded" offices, the Operations Officers, who were in charge of keys, had to be called constantly to unlock them. They even had to be called so that we could use the staff restrooms! What a mess!!

In addition, the roofs were leaking, not only on our house but all across the grounds! The gym roof was leaking as well and stayed that way for years. Patchwork was done to it, but no real repair. At times, buckets even had to be used to catch the excess rainwater dripping down from the ceiling, and then the Gym would be closed until all clean-up was done.

Another concern was directed at the building's exterior walls. Staff began noticing how they could see light coming in from the outside between the concrete blocks in several offices. It seemed as though someone had forgotten to use enough mortar when putting them in place. I actually saw these conditions for myself. They were real!

These noticeable conditions within the buildings led to inevitable questions such as: "Were the right materials used, or were shortcuts taken with too much of some things and not enough of others?" "Why were "window" air conditioners ordered when the windows were purposely constructed **not** to open?" and "Who had gotten this contract anyway since the quality of their workmanship appeared questionable?"

Unfortunately, this was not all! Rumors began spreading about the person in charge of finances getting kickbacks. The truth of this incident did come out, and the individual was soon moved to Central Office. Nothing was ever heard about the missing funds again.

Well, it wasn't long before we were informed that our first group of twenty boys would be arriving, and two weeks later, another twenty. This was a big shock because we were told that we could not bring any of our previous intake and processing materials with us or go back to Buckeye to get them. These records were to hold important information about each youth after conducting an in-depth interview with every one of them.

Now, our instructions are to "process" the new "in" coming youth and do their assessments by a given deadline and be on time for the next group. "But how could we proceed?" We thought, "Are we possibly being set up to lose our jobs?" I didn't think I was a "targeted" person, but I **was** part of the Substance Abuse Unit.

Anyway, I always kept extra forms in my briefcase for emergencies, and they came in handy right then. Great! We made copies, got all the youth processed, and had them ready for Substance Abuse classes.

Each department had an initial meeting with the Finance Committee. My Substance Abuse Team was allotted $6,000 for televisions, a video camera, videos, books, and other educational equipment. Soon classes started and became full. I kept waiting for our ordered equipment, asking and complaining about them until the Head of Finance finally told me that our items had never been ordered. When I asked, "Why?" She simply explained that she had spent the money! I was shocked. However, our Unit went on and managed with what little we had.

Everyone was busy trying to get settled in, filling up six Units within three Houses. Each House had two units assigned to them and named after trees. House One was designated, Ash and Elm. House Two's units were called Oak and Walnut, and House Three had units Maple and Hickory. Along with getting housing taken care of, other areas and responsibilities were being addressed at the same time. Social Workers were trying to get organized by meeting with their youth. The school had a new Principal that had never worked in the DYS system or with inner-city youth before, and the Recreation Department tried to keep the boys busy while waiting on the master schedule to be worked out.

Then, with everyone trying to adjust, we received word from downtown that we had **six** months to become the **first** Youth "Assessment" Center for the State of Ohio in Corrections! This news was startling to everyone. Yet, we had to meet the challenge and deal with the added pressure. Do it or don't have jobs! Central Office, many felt, had already known this information from the start.

The fact that the community of Cir had been misinformed about the facility initially became a big issue too. An Advisory Council was formed from various community leaders, including a Judge, Fire Chief, Adult Prison Chaplain, Pastors, and someone from the mayor's office, along with our Superintendent, Deputies, and Secretary. They met periodically at our location. I attended these meetings as well. The Superintendent always made sure to have light refreshments available for our guests, and the meetings would start after pleasantries were exchanged and agendas passed out. Old and new business was discussed, progress reports given, and available job openings mentioned.

One particular meeting got extremely heated because the community leaders stated that they were told that the Facility was going to be a "regular" high school, which it partly was. However, they **did not** know that it was to be a **leading** correctional institution for Ohio felons! They were very upset about this. They also stated that two hundred and sixty-six jobs had been promised to the people of Cir for allowing the Facility to be in their community.

Staff began to talk, and unions got involved because personnel struggled to make jobs available when there weren't many. The word went out that Central Office had not counted on the employees from Columbus to sign the transfer papers and travel thirty-two miles south to keep their jobs. But the majority did! Only some went to T.I.C.O. and Sci, another institution. This problem lingered for years, with many Black employees starting to get written up for petty things and some fired.

Veteran employees saw the firings as a way to create jobs for the community and began to speak out by making Staff and the Unions aware that they knew what was going on. One employee told the Union that he heard several Advisory Board members from Personnel say that "We only have to get rid of 100 more Blacks from Columbus, then we will be okay."

More trouble began to brew! New people were being hired and became Supervisors over veteran Staff with fifteen, twenty, or twenty-five years of experience. This was a dilemma because the "new" staff had **never** worked with felons from gang and drug dealer backgrounds. With the opening of any new facility, opportunities for higher level supervisory positions became available. Many of the Black Staff qualified, had experience, **and** college degrees from The Ohio State University,

Capital University, Wright State, and other surrounding universities. Yet, because of racially motivated practices, they felt that it would be useless to apply and not be selected, **or** they intentionally preferred to stay in their present positions.

One individual who felt this way was the Assistant Principal. I remember talking to him constantly about applying for the principal position because he had the experience **and** was the best person for the job. I was determined not to let him stay as the Assistant. I knew that God had opened the door for him to become the High School Principal at that time. When he finally and reluctantly applied, he got the job!

Several others that I began to talk to started applying for Unit Manager and Social Worker positions. However, the Personnel Office informed them that they did not qualify because they lacked a specific number of "points." The Office had not thoroughly explained how the application was based on a "points" system nor how "points" were given to fill out the paperwork properly. Applicants were to make sure that they had listed **all** types of their experiences working with youth, whether at school, church, youth groups, or other places. By showing many of my co-workers how to be more detailed on these forms, they started acquiring the required number of points to qualify for interviews and began to get higher-paying jobs when available.

Unfortunately, there were still times when African American employees had had more experience, education, and seniority, yet a position was given to a "new" person. I met with certain individuals and informed them to stand up for their rights and **not** just let things happen. - These veteran workers were then assisted by others, who had experienced similar situations. They received advice on how to proceed with getting a lawyer, making an appeal, and ultimately securing the jobs, they had qualified for.

12

Won't HE Do It!
The New Chaplain

*"Much prayer, much power! Little prayer, little power! No prayer, no power!" I heard the youth repeat, and I smiled. Words I had used to inspire them, I now heard them use to inspire. **God** was in control!*
– Pastor Richard Dyson/Edward McKendree Bounds

It was the first quarter of 1995 when I got a call from the Personnel Office to come in and talk with the Administrator. I was told that the Chaplain was retiring, and they were offering me the position. I readily agreed and signed the papers. He also informed me that I had been chosen from over two hundred applicants. I was happy and excited and felt honored to be the one selected. I knew that I was ready and fully prepared to serve the youth and Cir staff. The previous Chaplain had taken me under his wing, so to speak, and trained me in the many areas that I would be involved in. I was very grateful to him for seeing my true character and overjoyed that he had recommended me for the position.

I felt confident that I would be able to carry on what he had started. As the first African American Chaplain in the Department of Youth Services' history at the Cir facility **and** the first African American Seventh-day Adventist Juvenile Corrections

Chaplain for the State of Ohio, I knew that with God's help, all would be alright! These two milestone distinctions carried significant responsibility and weight to be successful, yet I rallied to the challenge.

The exceptional, professional education that I had received at Oakwood College along with my experiences working for Dr. E.E. Cleveland in the 1982 Canvas Cathedral Tent effort, which initiated the birth of the Columbus Central SDA Church, had been an integral part of my quality training. Additional preparation measures included working under Allegheny West Conference President, Pastor Henry M. Wright, who assigned me to assist Pastor James Best in conducting Revelation Seminars, workshops, and baptisms in the Columbus and Xenia areas. My committed involvement at the Ephesus SDA Church beginning in 1976 was also instrumental in providing a firm ministry foundation through Bible Study and Soul Winning training, serving as an active Elder for eight years, and leading out in other ministries.

Several of the "old timer" African American staff did not believe at first what they had heard about me acquiring my new position but hoped that it was true. These individuals had worked for twenty-five years or more in Corrections but had never known anyone of color to attain this type of position. They were sincerely proud of me and excited to witness new life and hope for the Department's future.

During my first week, I got a knock on my office door. A Caucasian man wanted to see who had gotten the position because he felt that the job was his. I had never seen him before nor knew anything about him. There was a little bitterness in his voice as he told me that he might as well leave the state and apply somewhere else. The next week, the same situation happened again, but this time by an African American Correction Officer.

I figured out that these guys were on third shift who had ministerial credentials and looking to take over the Chaplaincy position. However, I didn't let their visits bother me and instead started focusing on my goals.

My days started with my personal prayer to the Lord. I prayed and asked God what it was **He** wanted me to do with His incarcerated young men. He told me that, "They do not know Me and to **teach** them who I am." This instruction was all that I needed at the time. Then, I would check my e-mails, looking to see if any of the Social Workers had sent information concerning a youth for me to counsel because I had already let them know that I would be available to help them as well. Next, I would make my rounds in the school. The Teachers loved for me to stop in and observe or participate in whatever their classes were doing. Many times, the boys wanted me to see or hear about something that they had just finished. These accomplishments were just as meaningful for me as they were for them because they were like my sons, and I always tried to give them encouragement and hope.

I recall one of my first Church services and thought everything went well. I had a full house. We prayed, sang, and had what I thought was a good sermon. After releasing the boys, I returned to my office and prayed. God was **not** pleased and told me **not** to treat them like children but speak to them again. I immediately called them back in and preached this time the way God wanted me to do. When I finished, I had everyone circle up, and then I prayed aloud. The youth began to testify and opened up with their inner feelings. Some had tears in their eyes. The Correction Officer asked me what was going on because he was trying to maintain his composure, but he was crying and shaking too. The Holy Spirit had filled the room, touching, and embracing the service and these young men. What an awesome experience we had! Later, one young man that was holding my hand in the circle explained to me how another youth who was there had shot and killed his brother. He wanted to get revenge but said that as he listened to the message, the Lord touched him and told him to forgive the other youth.

Many of these young men, I found out, were in gangs and were rivals with each other, but the Lord had brought them together that day, and they had peace. After that, I knew God would always be there in the midst and in total control. He wanted me to know that these boys had lived lives of abuse, abandonment, and broken homes. They had been shot or shot at, exposed to gun fights, lived with older women at a young age, used drugs, partied, and woke up at home seeing a different man other than their father in and out of their houses. They had experienced things early in their lives that many of us never have. I was tough and firm, but most of all, they knew that I loved them.

Taking over as the new Clergy, I realized, would be very challenging. The institution had never had an African American as the Lead Chaplain before, and what I did or did not do would be under close scrutiny. At that time, the facility employed around two hundred sixty-six workers and housed approximately two hundred forty inmates. I knew that I had to build up my volunteer base because the former Chaplain had acquired fifteen to twenty regulars coming in on Sunday mornings. Now, only about four of them remained, and I had met three of the four. One was an elderly man who taught a Sunday School Bible class. He didn't like the way I was doing things at first. Soon afterward, though, his opinion of me changed because he came to some of my Church services and began to see what I was all about for himself.

The volunteers were used to doing services individually on the six units because no combined services were ever held.

However, my services were combined and conducted in the school's multipurpose room. In Columbus, there had been a separate Church building for services, but unfortunately, a Chapel had not been built at Cir. So, the school scheduled available times for the multipurpose room, and it was used for school activities Monday through Friday. Accessible times were reserved for me from 4:00 p.m. on weekday evenings and exclusively on Saturdays and Sundays. This arrangement was hard and very stressful, but I did not complain.

Chapel furniture and materials were kept in a classroom closet and only taken out on the weekends for Church. The sound equipment, keyboards, speakers, songbooks, and Bibles were kept there as well as additional chairs. All of these items had to be set up each week, along with rearranging the room's furniture. The pulpit was also stored on a flat dolly to transport it in and out quickly. I purposely came in early each week to make sure that things were in order and prepared so that services could run smoothly. Then, the boys could be at ease and become accustomed to how services would be conducted when they arrived. Otherwise, without structure and control, chaos could easily result.

One particular Sunday morning is a prime example. A faithful volunteer of mine brought in his friend to observe him in his Bible class. Later, they came over for me to meet him. As I was setting up for Church, putting out all the desks and chairs, the new gentleman made a comment about the number of chairs I had put out. He said, "Chaplain, you really have high expectations. You **really** don't need all of these desks and chairs." He got a good laugh out of that! However, I did not think it was funny. I told him to wait until I made the call and he'd see. When I had instructed the Operations Officer to make the call, this guest just happened to walk out into the hallway and looked at the line that kept going. He could not believe what he saw; one hundred twenty-five youth lined up for Church services! He was really shocked because he saw them for himself and screamed when he saw such a **long line** of boys that Sunday morning coming **excitedly** for Church. After that, **he** became a faithful volunteer!

I was confident in what I was doing because I always got my instructions from the Lord. The youth knew that I cared for them, and my schedule was set so that they saw me every day. Sometimes while visiting their units, I even had time to play card games and or corn hole with them. I also made myself available to the Correction Officers and listened to any problems they might be having with their groups or a particular youth.

They always knew that they could call or tell me about anything, and they did. The majority of the time, we would solve the problem right then. For instance, if a youth was having some type of immediate personal issue, the Officers knew not to let it fester.

Dealing with so many boys was challenging enough, and it didn't take much for someone to get on another's nerves. Trying to avoid potential situations that could easily cause arguments or fights was a much better strategy. So, I always told the Officers to let me know about things ASAP and made sure that each unit had "Request to see the Chaplain" forms readily available that were supplied and restocked by me personally.

Another part of my job was to contact any youth new to the facility and have a religious orientation session with him. The names of these boys were listed regularly. After checking my e-mails each week, I knew what youth came in and could schedule their individual meetings. A religious assessment would be completed, including information such as the religious affiliation of the youth and his parents, how often he attended Church during the last year, as well as the name of his Church and Pastor. The results showed that only about 10% of the parents considered themselves Church members. Most, however, were non-Church goers in their thirties and forties. The statistics, unfortunately, also concluded that about 99% of these young men never went to Church on a regular basis or had ever attended Church at all! Therefore, their religious affiliation responses reflected the persuasion of their parents or grandparents, mainly Baptist and Catholic. This questionnaire became a very helpful tool for me in deciding how best to serve each young person.

Besides completing a religious questionnaire during this time, the youth were advised how to contact me from then on with their concerns, problems, or emergencies. I explained how the Chaplain Request forms provided on Unit, were for counseling purposes. In dire emergencies, however, they were to ask their Correction Officers to call or page me immediately. Additional information concerning Church hours, special programs, and Bible Studies with volunteers was reviewed as well as how to sign out books in the religious library housed in my office. At the end of our meeting, I always gave them their own personal Bible and other encouraging reading materials. These positive strategies supported my youth ministry and were specifically designed to prevent and lessen potential peer conflicts.

Meeting the challenges of the prison environment was a day-to-day battle. Facing overcoming obstacles, defusing tense situations, and interceding in staff confrontations, all while letting God's light shine through me with a kind word, act, or deed, was the norm. I cannot stress enough how my prayer time **with God** made this possible because, in one's ministry things are never easy, the way it can sound. Satan will always attack and make things harder with conflicts, confusion, jealousy, hatred, and disagreements; whatever it takes for you not to succeed. The most painful, however, is when hindrances come from your **own** church family, Conference, and denomination.

I became an affiliated member of our denomination's Adventist Chaplaincy Ministries (ACM) organization, where Chaplains represented the military, collegiate, hospital, and prison arenas. Correctional Chaplains were instructed to introduce themselves to their own respective Churches and be available to serve in whatever capacity was needed. We were all members in good and regular standing, consistently supporting our Churches financially, and had vital experiences that would richly benefit each congregation. Our expertise in counseling, family member incarceration, and knowledge about many other issues would prove to be an invaluable asset. We anxiously waited to share and assist the Pastors. Yet, speaking for myself and other Chaplains, we were constantly viewed as "**invisible**."

For example, at my home church, I was never "acknowledged" or viewed as a genuine Clergyman, **but** I still continued serving as the Personal Ministry Director and Elder until I retired. When I would ask to do counseling workshops and interactive teaching seminars for the youth and interested parents, I was always denied. Invisible! Even though I'd been an active, participating member since 1976. I discovered that some of the younger Pastors coming into the ministry today have missed out on the "thorough" instruction available from the Pastors that I had come under. Men such as E.E. Cleveland, Henry Wright, E.C. Ward, C.T. Richards, Benjamin Reeves, and Calvin Rock taught integrity and were men of principle. Unfortunately, the younger guys, however, seem to be lacking in these areas. Some have large egos, and everything has to come from them **and** be about them because "**I**" am the "**Dr.**" much more than the Pastor of the Church.

Many do not want to hear what anyone else has to say or contribute and it seems that the Church administration has to be **their** way **or** no way! This is hurting our Churches, in my opinion.

At the Conference level, it appeared to be the same situation. I once tried to offer Substance Abuse Awareness training for the Pastors and Elders free of charge. I contacted our local Conference office and made an appointment to speak with the Conference President at that time to discuss the matter further. In addition to training ministers, my plan was to have counseling opportunities available for individuals and families during Camp-meeting in the summer because of the high incidence of teen drug use and prevalent crisis. Again, the answer was "No." Invisible! Members were looking for help as well as those in the community. This could have been a perfect opportunity for me to share and make a difference. The Conference **never** called me, **but** I did conduct "Drugs and the Family" awareness workshops **on my own** for receptive high schools and churches locally as well as in Florida, New Jersey, and Toledo and Springfield, Ohio.

The Conference mindset in denying my assistance was unfortunate. If we do not correct ourselves from jealousy and allow those with gifts and talents to use them for God's glory in the Church, the Church will not be as effective in spiritual warfare. We are to be **in** harmony, unified, and **working together** from the worldwide General Conference level, with its Divisions and Departments, right on down to the national and local levels of Church leadership. It's going to take men, women, and all of our youth to carry the Three Angels messages of Revelation fourteen, verses six to eleven, to the world using the gifts and talents God has given for the salvation of others and **for His glory**, not ours!

Now, I want to be careful in pointing out that there is a difference in being a Seventh-day Adventist Chaplain. God will use you and put you in unique situations to clarify both truth and light. There have been many times when He has opened up avenues or occasions for me to witness for Him. Once, when I went to the cafeteria to eat, I got my food and sat down. Another co-worker seated there began to ask me about eating pork. The whole table became silent, waiting on my answer. I knew that I had to tell the truth in a proper manner, not to offend anyone, **but** to explain what God's word said about eating and His health laws. God gave me the words to say, and I did share. Several individuals were impressed to know more, and I was able to show them the scriptural passages from the Bible later on that day. For others, who desired additional information, I gave The Amazing Facts pamphlet by Pastor Doug Bachelor on the health laws for them to read and study.

Later on, I found out that one of the youth happened to be talking to his teacher about what he was learning in Church. His Unit had heard a sermon I had preached on Daniel and the Three Hebrew Boys. They were very impressed by these Bible characters and their decision to follow God's health laws and not eat pork. Apparently, other youth in this same Unit had not only been intently listening to the sermon but influenced to start eating a healthier diet themselves.

At mealtimes, they began telling the cafeteria workers that they wanted brown bread, no Jello (because it contained pork), **and** no pork! The Cafeteria Director called me to her office and asked me how we could handle this "new" situation. After some discussion, it was decided that the cafeteria would provide brown bread for those who asked for it. In addition, if I signed a request form for any of them, they would be given another choice of meat besides pork and another snack besides

Jello. Those initial health changes led to our Cafeteria making other healthier choices too. For instance, they knew that I did not eat pork and began using vegetable oil for cooking instead of lard. Because of their diligence in being accommodating, willing to help, and food quality, our Cafeteria received top honors as **the** "Best Food Service" Department in D.Y.S.! Even the visitors who came to do ministry and out of state officials always praised the cafeteria on a regular basis for their food, including parents and special guests at our annual Christmas dinner.

Then, there were the times when all the Ohio State Chaplains met for quarterly meetings, and I would attend. We would have lunch together on occasion, and everyone would place their orders. I observed how many had eating habits that were somewhat out of control. Their choices mainly consisted of very large portions of pork and fish that one should not eat (seafood without fins and scales), plenty of coffee, soft drinks, and all followed by super-sized servings of dessert. After a while, they noticed that what I was eating was nothing like what they were having. I routinely got lemon water, little or no dessert, and never any pork products or seafood items that the Bible admonishes us not to eat.

One Chaplain, who was encouraged by my eating habits, asked if I could help him with his diet because he knew that I watched mine and was in good physical condition. I readily agreed and was glad to support him. From then on, when we ate out, the Chaplains would invariably talk about eating right and exercising because of my witness. During our Christmas gift exchange that year, I was able to give the Pastor, who had requested my help, a health-conscious vegetarian cookbook. He was ecstatic over it.

Another opportunity presented itself when I was asked to be the Guest Speaker at the Marysville Adult Women's

Reformatory in Marysville, Ohio. I arrived quite early Sabbath morning before I was scheduled to speak. The Chaplain invited me to sit in on the Prison Ministry Chaplaincy Seminar that she was co-hosting with Wright State University Professor Dr. Harold Trulear. Ten of his graduate students were there. The meeting went well and during the break, the Chaplain planned for us to have our lunch off grounds.

Afterward, I was to speak at 1 p.m. Unfortunately, due to time restraints, we were unable to go out as she had hoped and decided to order pizza instead. I was the only one that ordered a cheese pizza.

Everybody else ordered all types of meat, including pork pepperoni on theirs. When the pizza arrived, someone asked why I did not want any pepperoni pizza, and I told them. Everyone listened. Immediately the Professor quoted the text from Acts chapter ten, in the Bible, about God telling Peter to kill and eat whatever he wanted as long as he prayed. I let the Professor finish his main point while his entire class waited on my response. Very calmly, I tactfully presented the truth and stated, "I am familiar with the text, but if one would continued reading the **whole** chapter, you would find out that God was not talking about food, **but** He was referring to people, the Gentiles." I went on to explain that the health laws concerning foods could be found in the Book of Leviticus, the eleventh chapter, and Deuteronomy, chapter fourteen of the Bible.

It was amazing to me how impressed the Professor was and clearly in agreement with what I had said. He smiled. The conversation then changed to eating the proper foods and our bodies being God's temple. What was funny and so ironic seemed how the students started saying that they didn't **need** all that pepperoni. Instead, everybody began eating **all** of my cheese pizza. I started laughing with them and thought, "I'm just glad that I ordered an extra-large one." God is good! Our meal had become a Bible study.

After lunch, we all went to the Chapel, which was almost filled to capacity. There seated before us were about three hundred inmates. The entire graduate class and the Professor sat at my side to the left of the pulpit. Services were genuinely spiritual and very lively. The Chaplain was thrilled when everything was over that I had delivered a much-needed sermon that day, and the Professor with his grad students really thanked me for coming as well.

What happened afterward was very interesting and surprising! I got a letter from Dr. Trulear inviting me to be a chairperson on his committee helping his graduate students with first-hand Chaplaincy at my Institution. When the opportunity presented itself, he was able to bring them to Cir. I took them on a tour of the grounds explaining what I did daily; making rounds, stopping by to see youth at school and on units, checking on staff, and scheduling volunteer assignments and activities, among other things. The grad students were also able to observe an actual Church service and attend a workshop geared especially for them, including a question-and-answer session. This interaction proved to be very successful.

Now, Dr. Trulear wanted me to be part of a community, a holistic event involving the President of Wright State, parents of incarcerated youth, prominent Pastors of Dayton, Ohio, the media, including television coverage, and the Dayton Times. We met on the University's campus. I arrived early, which proved to be a blessing. Another gentleman, who was Muslim, and I began talking at the table. It appeared that everything had been set up for us. While we were talking, I happened to pick up a program and began to skim it. To my surprise, I read, **"Guest Speaker Chaplain James Benton.**" I was shocked! No one had sent me anything telling me that **I** was one of the two guest speakers, and **I** was to go first! What a shock!! You can only imagine how I felt.

The place began to fill up very quickly because news of this event had been heavily publicized in the Dayton area. Everybody there was very excited to finally come together and attempt to help young men who were falling by the wayside, going to prison instead of college. Probation Officers, Social Workers, Pastors, the College President, newspaper reporters, and the media were all there. I remember going to the restroom, washing my hands, and praying to God for His support because I was not prepared! When I finished my twenty to thirty minutes, people were standing and applauding me for my presentation. God had told me to just start talking about how I serve the Institution. I knew and shared statistics concerning the incarceration cycle whereby youth who didn't "know" their incarcerated fathers were now incarcerated fathers themselves and how **their** children wouldn't get to "know" them either. "No, we must break the cycle!"

God spoke through me that day! My remarks included pointing out to the audience that "When you are meeting people's needs, being there to hear what he or she has to say, listening and giving support, praying for and with someone, helping them not give up, **the love of God** is felt and seen. That makes **all** the difference in a person's life. They know God is real and that **you** really care."

I always carried a picture of Jesus Christ before a jail cell and kept extra copies to share at the institution. I would ask, "Is Jesus on the outside looking in or the inside looking out?" The answer I told them was both. In the Book of Matthew, chapter twenty- five verse forty-three, "When I was in prison ye visited Me not." The boys were told though by the Christian staff, community volunteers, **and** me that **God** loved them and that **He** cared! When the Conference was over, the

University President felt that it was fitting for me to give closing prayer, and I did.

Another time, a teacher got upset with the principal because he had had his staff attend an informative workshop given by an ex-homosexual. This presentation was essentially his testimony, reviewing how he had changed his life, how the pros and cons of his decision affected him, and how he overcame conflicts by accepting Christ as his personal Saviour. I had already heard the gentleman speak at one of the churches in the area. CYC had just become a "total" sex offender facility with a population of two hundred forty offenders. So, I invited him to come and do a workshop with my youth.

The principal sat in and thoroughly enjoyed it. He and I both felt that these types of programs would be most beneficial for his staff as well as for the boys.

Later on, the principal told me that he had gotten a call from Central Office because one of his teachers had put in a complaint about being mandated to attend this particular workshop. She felt personally offended by the presenter mentioning Jesus' name, and she did not want to hear that because it was against her religion. Yet, for over the twenty years that we had known her, she had **never** done anything like this before.

Her complaint about religious liberty rights led to a situation that grew larger and larger. The Principal, Warden, and Central Office became involved and the Governor's Office also. Sessions were held several times, with the principal meeting DYS officials and a representative from the Governor's Office to discuss the matter. An investigation was conducted and uncovered that the complaining Teacher, one week prior to the workshop, had become involved in a "new," unheard-of religion that did not believe in Jesus Christ. This is probably why she felt so offended. However, many others, especially Christians, who **do** follow Jesus, were upset when word spread around the institution about **her** charges. I was affected as well because **I** was the Chaplain who had invited the speaker to come in the first place and the religious leader of the facility.

The incident eventually impacted **all** Chaplains in Ohio because it was resolved by stipulating that Chaplains could **no** longer pray using Jesus' name alone! I was informed by the principal and our "Lead" Chaplain, a communications spokesperson from downtown, that this decision was final **and** to be upheld. None of the Chaplains nor myself, unfortunately, were given a chance to express **our** religious perspective on the dilemma to the officials **or** give any input on how we felt about what procedures needed to be in place from then on for similar situations.

This occurrence happened while the school was scheduling graduation. The principal would invariably ask me to pray at the event. I told him that if I could not use the name of Jesus, there would be no need for me to pray. I told him, "If you call me, I will call on the name Jesus despite whatever directives were mandated because I was dedicated to the Lord."

The day of the graduation was beautiful. It was always held outside with special guests including parents, Central Office representatives, friends, judges from the community, and other public officials attending. When I got to work that morning, the principal came to my office and informed me that he had thought of a way to handle the "prayer" situation. He was going to have three youth open the ceremony. They did so, and **they** began with prayer! These young men testified about the Lord Jesus Christ and how **if** it were not for Him, they would **not** have made it. These youth also stated that through "much prayer, one had much power," "little prayer, little power," "no prayer, no power," and how they had learned about Jesus Christ at Church with Chaplain Benton every week. That was amazing!

No one could say a word. The audience applauded loudly, and the event was a big success. The graduating **youth** testified about Jesus Christ and what prayer had done for them! I sat there overwhelmed with joy as I witnessed the power of God and how **He** is always there for us, especially when we stand up for Him and His Holy Word. What ended up coming down from the Governor's Office then was that we were to recognize all other faiths in silent prayer first. **Then**, we could **end in Jesus' name**. This official word on "prayer" protocol was eventually sent to all Ohio Chaplains so that no one of varying faiths would feel offended.

...it is good for me to draw near to God: I have put my trust in the Lord GOD,...
-Psalm 73:28

Generation X - Young Minds Under Attack

There is a way which seemeth right unto a man, but the end thereof are the ways of death.

Proverbs 14:12, KJV

When looking back at the early 80's and 90's, in general, I began to see a drastic change in youth. However, in my opinion, young people are not totally to blame for their attitudes and behaviors. Priorities in this country changed, and I feel that societal factors played a major role in how many of them turned out. They were negatively affected by the music of the "hip hop" generation, and "rap" music was constantly featured on radio stations with filthy lyrics about young girls, drugs, and sex. The movie industry also bombarded them with motion pictures glorifying sex, murder, drugs, and crime.

Violence on the streets became more common place as the availability and accessibility of guns prevailed, and the ease of acquiring crack cocaine on street corners in the "hood" or even "delivered" to predominantly wealthy areas of town was on the rise.

Schools, on the whole, did not have control of the youth either. Once considered "safe" havens for our sons and

daughters, our schools have instead become more challenging and confrontational arenas. Students were seemingly
allowed to wear and do just about anything imaginable
because numerous teachers and principals were afraid of
them. The same "glorified" negative elements highlighted
in the media were reflected in youth attitudes and actions
because young people nowadays seem so easily misled and
skeptical about trusting those who have proven themselves
to be trustworthy.

Some use hate and bullying tactics to deal with their
own insecurities, which has led to these conditions becoming major issues at schools. Many youth have been injured
from fights, and some have even lost their lives because no
one has "stepped" up to say anything about altercations or
make recurring problems known, prevented, and dealt with.
Unfortunately, some victims have even taken the situation into
their own hands by bringing weapons to school. One probably preventable incident occurred in the fall of 2011. During
a middle school assembly on the West side, one youth came
from behind and slit the throat of another boy, the "bully,"
who had been harassing him every day! The "bullied" youth
said that nobody was doing anything about the situation. This
issue of "bullying" has gotten so out of hand now that it will
take **everyone**: parents, schools, churches, the media, **and** law
enforcement alike coming together to help end these violent
acts.

The popularity of partying on college campuses and "spring
break" flings in Florida, the Caribbean, Mexican beaches, and
elsewhere continued exploiting "fun." Marijuana and using
other drugs, alcohol, sex, and partying all day and night were
considered the norm. Wanting to fit in and be accepted by
their peers, the majority of young people thought that they
would be missing out on all the "fun" that they perceived all

the other youth appeared to be having. So, they would join in by smoking marijuana and participate in dangerous drinking and pill-popping games at parties just to be "cool" and a part of the excitement. Tragic stories, however, did happen! Consequences were never really considered or thought about. Many times, as a result of these escapades though, lives were adversely affected, disrupted, and even deaths occurred with them usually being downplayed, infrequently heard about, or never told. Yet, the beat goes on. Scripture in Proverbs 14:12 tells us, *There is a way which **seemeth** right unto a man; but the end thereof are the ways of death.*

Consider *"a partial day in the life of Cir youth"*:

It was a beautiful spring day, about 77 degrees. The sun was shining and as I walked outside on grounds, I noticed a Unit of boys playing softball at the softball diamond.

They were fooling around and not taking anything about the game seriously. I was somewhat bothered by their actions because I had grown up playing this game with my brothers. I loved sports and always considered them important because others had taken their time to teach me "how" to play. Sports kept me out of trouble, and baseball was fun!

I had the Correction Officers in charge of these boys challenge another Unit to an actual game. I was the umpire, standing behind the fence of home plate, calling balls and strikes. As I watched though, I made some shocking discoveries. The boys did not know **how** to hold a bat or even hit the ball! They got angry with their **own** teammates easily, putting each other down, and heckling whoever was up at bat from their **own** team! I had never seen anything like it.

I saw them pick up the baseball gloves and go out onto the playing field. One particular player looked at the glove as if he'd never seen one before. I asked him that question, and he said, "No." Sometimes the boys had them on backward or even had a left-handed glove on their right hand. This was really sad to see because there was a time in our country, the USA, when baseball was considered "the sport" of sports.

Baseball and apple pie were the greatest! Little boys just naturally grew up playing little league baseball. What happened? The negative elements mentioned previously have deprived these youth of what was once considered common and everyday.

As I said earlier, the blame for youth attitudes and wayward behaviors cannot all be put on them. Society changed due to various components coming into play over the last two decades. Consider the breakdown of the family, for instance. I really believe that satan, also called the devil, has wholeheartedly directed a special attack on the family unit. Mothers had to raise their children with the father in jail, M.I.A., "Missing in Action," or possibly some on crack leaving their children behind to care for themselves without any parental guidance. Then, there are those men who have fathered a child or children, feel no obligation to them, and do **not** pay child support. Mothers are left to struggle with the responsibility of trying to feed and support their families by themselves. The father is **not** there, and everyone is affected. Daughters may seek love in all the wrong places just to feel special; instead of being made aware of their true, intrinsic value by a loving, nurturing father. In addition, drugs are readily available, and with these multiple components coming together, a toll has been taken on our younger generations. These conditions, though, should not easily take a Christian by surprise because the Bible has predicted how these same perilous times would be a part of the last-day events of earth's history.

Another major factor to consider is technology. New inventions, like the computer chip, social media formats, video games, and numerous handheld technological devices, are very influential. These items were and are fantastic when used in positive ways.

However, they can be very detrimental. For example, sitting for eight or more hours constantly playing video games, participating in cyberbullying, conversing with strangers in "chat" rooms of questionable sites, watching pornography, buying illegal weapons, or being lured to meet strangers who are predators and or sex offenders have lasting impacts. The Bible says, "Love not the world, neither the things that are in the world. If any man love the world, the love of the Father is not in him. For all that is in the world, the lust of the flesh and the lust of the eyes, and the pride of life is not of the Father, but is of the world." I John 2:15-16. When we get caught up in all of these worldly things, we lose sight of our own salvation and God. Consequently, we are lured away into sin with the desires of the flesh and sinful habits.

The world has become pleasure and entertainment crazy! Today, there are fantastic offers for weekend "get-aways"; enticing and convenient gambling trips to Las Vegas, Atlantic City, or other places, all promising to have one back home in time for work Monday morning. In addition, our TVs are bombarded with all kinds of reality shows, commercials, witchcraft, spiritualism, and R-rated movies, that in my opinion, have definitely played a large part in negatively influencing young minds. Events that were once considered risqué, and should still be, are no longer viewed as such but are now regarded as passé or acceptable. Viewers' minds are being saturated with disturbing situations, subliminal messages, and images dulling an individual's senses to the point where these things are no longer thought of as abnormal or anything to be "**that**" concerned about!

Lastly, I would like to reiterate how the incarcerated youth nor their parents were "Church" goers and generally reflect mainstream America. I have found, through my ministry, that only a small percentage of Americans attend church regularly, especially from our larger cities. Their focus and preferences seem to be primarily directed towards deriving satisfaction from worldly things and **not** through God and His word.

Facebook, Twitter, and connecting through cell phone messages and texting have become standard ways of interacting. Getting to know one's neighbors or playing outside with friends as I did when growing up isn't usually done anymore where we spoke face-to-face. Valuable lessons such as trust, integrity, and companionship, I feel, have been lost as a result of these more impersonal, non-verbal communication methods utilized today and a lack of spending "fun" times together. People having a connection with the Lord is also vital, to me, in giving one hope, showing love, staying positive, and learning coping skills with our day-to-day challenges.

Putting Out Fires

...I found that God used me to be the mediator, the 'buffer', the one who could by His strength, grace, and mercy redirect 'fire' situations and put them out.

My daily routine included visiting the cafeteria, not always to eat, but also having an opportunity to check on the staff there. Periodically, problems would come up dealing with a youth and or certain employees. The Cafeteria Director would, in turn, call me in privately to discuss these situations and possible solutions. She always requested prayer for herself and her entire department. Asking for counseling for her team and their families was important to her, and I made myself available to them because I knew that she really cared.

One intervention that readily comes to mind is when I was called to the cafeteria, where two workers were heatedly arguing back and forth. One worker had grabbed a butcher knife while screaming back at the one screaming at her. As I entered the building, I couldn't help but overhear them and quickly went into the kitchen to help calm them down. One of the cooks was already able to get the knife away from Ms. M., and the situation was diffused. The circumstances still ended up stressing out the other workers for the rest of that week, and everyone on the grounds still heard about it.

The woman who was threatened wrote a complaint. Ms. M. got sent home without pay and was almost fired! The Cafeteria Director called me in, gave me some insight into the whole situation, and asked for my help. She didn't want either woman to be fired because both were good workers. I asked to talk to Ms. S. and found out that the problem was coming from working long hours, pressure from being in a very small kitchen, and lack of communication with "too many" trying to be in charge! I was also able to talk to Ms. M. over the phone and eventually found out that this was the root of the problem for her too.

I informed the Cafeteria Director of their concerns, and changes were made. The working conditions improved, and a more pleasant atmosphere was felt. Workers were able to make suggestions in writing, and communication between employees got better too. Soft, inspiring music was played during their working hours, and I was asked to visit them on a regular basis. I made it a point to stop by the kitchen and talk with everyone.

Having their day run smoothly was important because they were responsible for preparing countless breakfasts, lunches, dinners, and snacks for the entire inmate population. This task was stressful enough without adding bickering among themselves. Keeping the daily routine operating efficiently was vital because **if** meals weren't ready **or** on time, the entire schedule for the institution would be out of sync, and riots could easily break out. Things, however, really did change for the better. New pictures were even hung on the walls making the dining area more inviting and an improved, positive setting.

Getting back to the two women arguing and on the verge of a serious altercation, I was able to talk with the Administration about them. Together we came up with a plan for Ms. M.

that included her taking anger management classes with me for two weeks.

Later on, she and the other worker made up and hugged one another in my presence after she apologized to her supervisor and coworker. Ms. M. did not get fired after twenty-two years of service and went on to retire. Both women remained good friends and coworkers. Sometimes it only takes a little time and care to really see what's behind a situation like this one.

So many things happened during those years. It seemed like I was always called on to put out "fires," or in other words, "trouble," mainly between Staff. I did not mind, but one would think that these professionals already knew how to handle disagreements between themselves. However, this was not the case. We had individuals in various careers with professional status and top-paying jobs. Yet, many were not conducting themselves in a noticeably "professional" manner with their actions. I always wanted everyone to get along and cooperate, especially for the sake of the youth. They needed to see positive examples set before them. As a result, I found that God used me to be the mediator, the "buffer," the one who could, by His strength, grace, and mercy redirect "fire" situations and put them out. I also hoped that the Institution could possess a pleasant, peaceful atmosphere, even though it was a correctional facility. Day by day, moment by moment, my prayers ascended for God to grant that this would be so.

The LORD is good to all: and his tender mercies are over all his works.
-Psalm 145:9

15

Community Mentors & Innovative Speakers

"Chaplain, who do you go to for help when you need it? Because you seem to be there for everybody. It seems to be overwhelming!" I chuckled a bit at first, being surprised that she was so in tune knowing how it could be."
— *Kentucky State University female student*

During the early years, back in the mid and late 90s, I knew that I had to go into the community and make myself more visible there. I needed to meet the people of the area and establish a viable relationship with them first before hoping for their desire or commitment to volunteer at the Facility. Reaching out to store owners, retail workers, school principals, funeral home directors, barbershops, car dealerships, adult prison officers, among others, and local law enforcement became my priority.

Eventually, I became good friends with the Common Pleas Court Judge. As a result, he started volunteering on a regular basis conducting Bible Studies with the boys every Sunday. The Fire Chief also became a regular Sunday volunteer and served as an honored speaker at one of our Volunteer Banquets. I made sure to visit the Cir Bible College campus frequently and gave on-site volunteer orientation classes. Anyone who wanted to become a volunteer for the Institution was given official training by me at that time. These volunteers, from the community at large and from the college, were valuable assets enriching the lives of our incarcerated ones.

The Cir Bible College (renamed Ohio Christian University, 2006) students and staff alike always played a vital role in partnering with us. Their choirs performed several concerts over the years, and their staff had multiple assemblies. Some of the programs dealt with the importance and benefits of having a college education. Individual students also testified how college had changed their lives.

Besides helping coach the correctional basketball team, I made a point of attending a number of the College's games. I met the players and their coaches. In time, we developed a genuine friendship, and because of it, I was able to establish a Basketball Mentoring Program with them. This planned arrangement allowed personal interaction between the two teams. The College team would come over, and meetings were held prior to actually playing any games. Each session began with prayer. Then, I would have the Coach enlist his players to give personal testimonies. Afterward, my youth would do the same. This was a powerful way of allowing the young men to be honest and open with one another. My boys got a chance to see and hear firsthand what making the right choices was all about, as well as what it was like to work through hard times and obstacles to become successful. On the other hand, the college youth got to see and hear about what it was like when wrong decisions were made, and landed behind bars. Both sides became better acquainted and soon the students even became volunteer mentors and positive role models for my youth. Our sessions closed with prayer, and then, game time!

Taking the college team on a tour of the Institution and letting them see what being incarcerated was like firsthand, uncut, was the program's second component. It gave them a real "taste" of prison life. I showed them the living quarters, the "Isolation" Room (used for those out of control or fighting), and other areas on the grounds. The program was very successful, and we always thanked the College President, his Staff, Basketball Coach, and players for everything they were doing for us.

In addition to this specific program, our Institution featured a "Touring" Mentoring Program set up with OSU that allowed students majoring in Social Work, Criminal Justice, and Ministry to do internships with our Social Workers and me. Our Y.E.T., Youth Engagement Team, was in charge of scheduling, and students were assigned by their professors and me to work with our Social Workers during weekdays. After completing their pre-determined set of coursework hours, college credits would be given. This volunteer base was not only local but spread to include students from Wright State, Kentucky State, Paine University, and Capital University.

Auxiliary informational tours were also conducted by the Administration. As soon as students arrived, the Superintendent would be introduced. Then, the Operations Department would explain how the entire grounds and Institution were monitored from their extensive system of cameras. Next, stops would be made to the Nurses Station, Cafeteria, Housing Units, and the Lock Up "Isolation" Room. Finally, the students would visit the High School complete with its printing and computer areas, regular classrooms, and library. Even though I was usually busy making rounds when these tours were conducted, I was always introduced to the groups and still took time to talk with them, answer questions, and welcome them to the Facility.

One of the most memorable times was when the Recreational Director arranged for thirty students from his alma mater, Kentucky State University, to come. My Y.E.T. members had planned a big day for them, and the Institution was very excited about their visit. Upon arrival a tour of the facility was given and at a designated time, they were taken to the library for a "Q and A" period. Individual Staff had been asked to highlight specific aspects of their jobs as well as share the requirements and educational preparation necessary for each career. Social Workers, Teachers, Correction Officers, Nurses, Maintenance, Administrators, Secretaries, and I, as Chaplain, were present.

When it was my turn to speak, I reviewed and explained all of my duties. One young lady was impressed to ask, "Chaplain, **who** do you go to for help when you need it? Because you seem to be there for everybody, it seems to be overwhelming!" I chuckled a bit at first, being surprised that she was so in tune knowing how it could be, and then answered, "**God**, The Father."

Afterward, we all enjoyed a special lunch prepared by the cafeteria and then went to the Gym for a Fellowship Social with the inmates. Our youth were excited for this time to actually talk with "college" students, especially the young women, and ask them about college life. At the end of the day, everyone met up front in the Visitation area to recap. The KSU youth were able to comment or ask any other questions that they hadn't had an opportunity to ask directly to the Superintendent. The youth had very positive things to say about the Facility and were impressed to see how we ran a prison. They said that it seemed more like a school atmosphere even though the young men were locked up. We concluded by taking pictures next to the Kentucky State bus in front of the institution.

Outside of the job, I was drawn to a basketball organization that I heard about called First Team. This dedicated group of Christian men mentored youth about life using Biblical principles. I became their volunteer Chaplain because I loved seeing kids involved in sports and being physically active while at the same time learning about the Lord. We were located in the Columbus community, teaching basketball skills, and held camps throughout the city every summer. Our focus was on mentoring children and teens from seven to eighteen, especially ones from the inner-city, all year round.

Former NBA star and Ohio State legend Clark Kellogg was one of our Board members. Ironically, one day, a youth at work asked me, "How come I never did a camp with them at the prison?" Since I was always with them, I had never thought about doing one. I prayed about it and felt led to plan a basketball camp there through the Recreation Department. One of the First Team Coaches came and helped out for three evenings during the week. Every youth at the Institution wanted to sign up, but I could not allow specific Housing units to participate.

Those who were currently on a medical restriction, not attending school, or on "House" restrictions could not participate either.

The Camps were a big hit at the Gym. Not too long after that, around 2004, I was asked by the Recreation Director to come to his meeting to discuss with D.Y.S. officials how we could continue to keep the boys actively engaged. We suggested, "Let's have Basketball Teams at each Facility. Have a Team with Try Outs and follow the same basketball rules as the Ohio high schools do". We continued to meet over the next six months and eventually started the D.Y.S. Basketball League, with each institution having a team with uniforms and official State of Ohio referees to officiate.

All of that eventually led me to become an Assistant Coach and later Head Coach over the next six years. We had Cu, InR, Ma, Sci, Cir, PaCr, and ORVa, to mention most of the teams. Scrimmages were played with various community and church teams throughout the state, as well as colleges. Over time, the Superintendents, Teachers, and Staff became involved by supporting their teams and came to the games held in the evenings. The Superintendents even began bragging about **their** teams and started walking and talking with a "new" swagger when mentioning **their** facilities in meetings they had together. The League was a success!

As the years passed, I began to invite former N.B.A. players to come and speak to the boys. I contacted Mr. "Special K," Clark Kellogg, who said that he would be delighted to come. I was really impressed with him because he never asked for a fee and came for morning Church Services where he shared his personal testimony about his life, God, and basketball. After lunch, he stayed, and we did another Camp. He signed and passed out over 240 tee shirts that day!

Whenever I called Clark, if he didn't have any other pressing engagements, he would come and do the same format again, staying and socializing with the youth and Staff alike. During these visits, the youth got to see him up close and personal. They loved him and were thrilled that he played basketball with them, took pictures, and stayed all day. He really knew what that would mean to someone incarcerated, and he knew that maybe he could plant a seed in their hearts that God would water.

Another OSU star and former NBA player that I had to come in and bless our youth was Lawrence Funderburke. He told them about his life growing up with all of its ups and downs and how he overcame obstacles from his rough neighborhood life.

Lawrence spoke about his latest book, <u>Triangle</u> <u>Formula</u> <u>of Success</u>, and conducted a workshop for about 140 boys that day. The staff as well as the youth that came to the assembly were thrilled to meet and listen to him speak. We purchased copies of his book, and I made sure that each youth got one. An additional copy was placed in the school library.

Mr. Larry Jones, a graduate of East High School, Columbus, Ohio and an ABA Basketball star, came to see us as well and held shooting workshops for the Basketball Team. He, too, spoke about life as a new player and temptations that come into one's life. The youth enjoyed Larry and were intrigued by him because he challenged them to a fifteen-foot to twenty-foot jump shot contest with the best out of fifteen shots. He played fourteen guys on the team, one by one, and defeated each player that same night! He showed them newspaper clippings of several scoring records that he held while playing in the early 1970s. They were excited to meet him and to have his autograph.

My motivational sports figures lineup also included professional NFL football player Siran Stacy. He was a star at the University of Alabama and the number two draft choice in 1992. He played for the Philadelphia Eagles. He came and presented his real-life story in a very moving and inspiring way. The youth were impressed and enjoyed him a lot.

Another method that I used to keep the youth mentally motivated, was by inviting other ministry groups to come in and share their stories. One group was led by Bill Glass, former Cleveland Browns football great Tight End that had played and retired from the NFL. Mr. Glass started the "Weekend of Champions." This weekend involved bringing professional athletes in basketball, baseball, football, college players, singers, and volunteers from around the U.S. to the prison for a full three day event. They told about their individual lives, both good and bad, and especially how God came into their hearts when they accepted Him as their personal Saviour. It was a blessing for us to host this special weekend on more than one occasion and see God use the positive, changed lives of those celebrities who came.

Each time I had a stage set up because Bill's organization was very sharp and synchronized. We would meet several months in advance with them. Afterward, I'd schedule the weekend activities and meet with Security, Cafeteria staff, and Unit Managers so that everyone would be notified and ready. The event was always held outside with microphones, speakers, and assigned seating for our six Housing Units. The youth were thrilled to hear stories and watch various demonstrations by different speakers. One champion tore a whole telephone book in half while quoting Bible scriptures. Another team member from the famous Melendez family walked on a highwire tightrope quoting Scripture while balancing a chair on his head. The boys also witnessed other unparalleled strength and endurance when a steel frying pan was easily bent into a tubular shape, a baseball bat was broken over a player's thigh, and a thick iron bar was bent in half. All honor and praise were given to the Lord for these feats. What a tribute to God!

Trust in the LORD, and do good:...
-Psalm 37:3

16

Sex Offenders

*"What do you think **I** was doing when I sat with sinners and outcasts? I ate at their homes and let them know that I cared about them and loved them. I was always in their midst and walked among them. If **you** don't, **how** will they ever know **who I am** if they do not see it in **you**, son?"*

round 2001, we switched from operating as the Reception Center to becoming **the** designated "sex offender" Institution. Our whole atmosphere changed. A depressing, ominous spirit seemed to permeate everywhere. Staff began complaining more and more about being overwhelmed. They found themselves entirely backed up with their youth assessments, and Social Workers got stressed out. Some of them, along with other personnel, came to see me. We talked at length about their frustrations and other feelings they were now experiencing. Everyone felt that "we" had been pressed into this new service role **without** being properly trained.

For you see, every youth coming to us had to go through an in-depth Orientation. These procedures included being completely assessed by various staff **and** myself along with assigning them to a Social Worker. At first, the boys were being sent to Cir about ten at a time. This was a manageable number for us to process and work with. Soon afterward, however, they were being transported more rapidly, with fifteen to twenty coming every week! This accelerated number of inmates continued, arriving at that rate until the entire two hundred forty youth were transferred regardless of our inability to keep up with processing such large numbers of boys at one time.

Sex offenders, we found out, had a variety of **other** psychological problems **along** with being sex offenders, making them difficult to deal with. For instance, some had ADHD syndrome, drug addiction, mental problems, mental and physical abuse issues, sexual abuse, and so forth. Many were on psychiatric medications. I was totally unaware and shocked to find out from our Nurses that **any** youth could refuse their prescriptions **if** they wanted to. A number of times, after finding out that taking "meds" was optional, boys started refusing them even more. For the safety of **all** workers, being made aware of such pertinent information was imperative because those same ones who refused meds posed a potential risk to everyone else by possibly losing their tempers and "going off"!

During that 2001-2002 time period, one particular youth who came to us from Sci seemed to mesmerize the others. They ranted and raved about his coming and viewed him as a "god," their hero, and leader. Whatever he said, they would believe and do. I found out that youth even began pretending to take their meds, hiding them under their tongues instead of swallowing them. A.T., their infamous leader, had over forty boys transporting these meds during school hours from youth to youth, eventually returning to him. He was slick enough to never get caught with any pills himself but had his followers keep two large bags of the stuff in their rooms.

Operations/Security Correction Officers conducted unannounced inspections along with Unit Officers. They found a large bag of over 400 psychotropic pills that A.T. was selling and using to bargain for sexual favors or anything else his crew wanted. The youth **never** told that their hero was responsible.

This incident was definitely an "eye opener" for the entire prison. I went to the Superintendent, the Union rep, and the Administration to inform them about the effect and problems that this "rush of service" had put on everyone. The Administration listened and acquired one week of mandatory professional training classes for all staff. But by then, we needed more than one week! We needed more classes with continual counseling instruction to follow. The change was very difficult for all.

Well, it wasn't long after the sex offenders arrived that additional incidents began to happen. In the school, on the Units, in back hallways, in the gym, and wherever, these boys were performing all types of sexual acts with one another. We were extremely shocked because none of us, except for a few, had ever worked with sex offenders before. One Social Worker told me that she had **just** transferred to our Facility to get away from them because she couldn't take the association and mental stress that it takes to work with sex offenders. She got another job and left.

Sometimes you hear things, and it becomes hard to imagine that they are really taking place. I became surprised and angry because staff and Administration began to act like the youths' blatant sexual behavior was a common, everyday occurrence. To me, it was an abomination, repulsive, and offensive that should be dealt with harshly. Young boys just coming into the Facility put into cells with older, more aggressive young men should not be, but it seemed that no one saw this arrangement as a problem or even cared.

Some of these guys, most of the time, had never had any experience with sex until they were "groomed" by these aggressive, older boys. However, once these younger boys had experienced sex with the older ones, and even though they would feel bad and know that they did something wrong; in their minds, down deep, they would believe that this was what sex is all about and adopt an "I hate it," "I love it" mentality.

"I don't want to date girls," one boy said to me. "I like boys." I felt that his comments were satanic because they reminded me of vampire movies where vampires would bite innocent victims, and later the victims became vampires too! Many of these youth were proud and did not hide what they were or had become. Several would act out and tell staff what they liked and preferred in relationships. They had boyfriends and were always passing notes in school throughout the school day. These boys even thought that this would be an "easy" way to communicate during Church as well, only to find that their notes **were** intercepted by the Correction Officers!

I continued to teach God's word at our Church Services and maintained the standard of the husband and wife, male and female companionship model. In this way, the young men's choices never "totally" took over the Institution. Being seen and heard, I felt, was the best example for the boys to gain an understanding of **God's design** because "one's actions **do** speak louder than words." Several of our dedicated staff and volunteers that were good, Christian family men at home, on the job, and in their communities exemplified those who went out of their way to help society be a better place. **Their** witness and positive influence, especially at Cir, was a strong voice **for** God.

Soon I began realizing that youth, in general, were being "swayed" to be involved in damaging sexual behaviors. It seemed as if no one was talking about these new "turn- ons," but young people were well aware of them. For example, one particular Sunday afternoon, the prison ministry group from a prominent church in the city came at their scheduled time.

Their team consisted of the youth pastor, singers, and sometimes even a praise team. These blessed, trained, and dedicated young people had been working with us for over five years. They were always prepared, and performed excellent, relevant skits and we looked forward to having them.

In preparing for their visit, I would set up the chapel area for the service, complete with the sound system, adequate seating, and music. Then, I would escort the team from the Front Desk back to where we would be worshipping and call for about thirty to forty- five youth to participate. The majority of these boys were the young men who had already attended morning Services and were serious about studying the Bible and learning to know Jesus for themselves. The ministry team and inmates alike were excited. I purposely sat in the back where I could see and hear everything easily. Services were always very uplifting and full of the Holy Spirit.

That day, the young minister, "D", gave a testimony about being unhappy at one point in his life. When he finished telling his story, I sat there in disbelief and amazed at what I had just heard. He spoke about how one of his male friends had approached him and told him that his secret desire was to have sex with him. "D" said that he didn't answer this guy right away because his words were totally unexpected. His friend had no regard for his being in the ministry or his marriage. But eventually, "D" began to think about this proposition and said, "Yes." "What?" I thought. I was dumbfounded! "This type of behavior coming out of a "Christian" High School setting! What's going on?"

"D" had seemed so strong in the Lord, to me, really aspiring, intelligent, and unwilling to compromise God's word or His standard. However, his "turn-on" decision held painful consequences. "D" told us about the depression and inner conflict that plagued him afterwards and also of his inability to tell his wife what he had done. Furthermore, he had prob-ably now damaged his chances of pastoring a large congrega-tion sometime in the future.

Secretly young people already knew about these types of sexual "turn-ons" for kicks. When I began asking youth what they knew about these things, they did not hesitate to tell me about the new "thrill" games going on and considered com-monplace in public schools. Dares were being played out, hav-ing oral sex under stairways and morning sex before classes were acts viewed by them as typical. Girls kissing other girls, two together or in group circles, and boys with boys became the ultimate turn-on. These unacceptable behaviors were all taking place right here at work, in churches, and in public schools. But, most disturbing to me was how none of the churches or news media were addressing the issue!

Other alarming situations were not only taking place with youth, but many cases involving adults engaged in sex-ual misconduct and abusing minors began to be publicized around the country as well. One of the most shocking stories came out in 2010 about charismatic Bishop Eddie Long, Pas-tor of the New Birth Baptist Church in Atlanta, Georgia. Six young men alleged that he had sexually abused them when they were teens. Four were members of his church.

One young man, Maurice Robinson, stated that the minis-ter would often take him on trips when he was fifteen. They would travel to New Zealand, and Long would engage in sexual acts with him there. This information became national news; broadcasted on radio, television, and over the internet. This Pastor's church was definitely affected and split over the controversy. Many members left in anger and disgust. Eventu-ally, his wife of twenty-one years and mother of their four chil-dren filed for divorce December 24 of that same year. Bishop

Long always denied the allegations but in May 2011, he settled out of court for an undisclosed sum.

Years ago, news reports also accused Catholic priests of molestations and being in sexually abusive relationships with young boys. Today, even greater numbers of such abuse cases involving them are surfacing and coming to the forefront from everywhere!

Then, there's the biggest child abuse scandal to come out at a major "Big Ten" school, Penn State University. Their former Assistant Football Coach, Jerry Sandusky, was indicted for sexual misconduct. He was charged in 2011 with fifty-two counts of child molestation dating from 1994 to 2009 and according to Wikipedia, the free encyclopedia, even as far back as the 1970s. On October 9, 2012, the courts found Sandusky guilty on forty-five of forty-eight counts of sexual abuse. Four counts were dropped.

However, he was sentenced to serve a minimum of thirty years and a maximum of sixty years in prison. His unacceptable behavior had far-reaching outcomes on the University also. On July 23, 2012, the NCAA imposed ongoing penalties on Penn State's athletic program. Penalties that included a sixty-million dollar fine, four-year past season ban, and the vacating of all victories from 1998 to 2011. The Big Ten Conference imposed an additional thirteen-million dollar fine plus a loss of forty scholarships from 2013 to 2017 and other sanctions. The penalties were some of the most severe rulings to ever be imposed on a college program.

Unfortunately, the student body was adversely affected as well because they loved their Head Coach, Joe Paterno, who was implicated in knowing about his Assistant's actions yet did nothing to correct the situation. On July 22, after local organizations complained, the school decided to take down the legendary statue of Paterno at Beaver Stadium. Many civil lawsuits resulted against the University because of Jerry Sandusky's sexual activities and against others who knew about it and had turned away in denial.

Sin is devastating! One man's wrongdoings cause a ripple effect on others. People's lives are touched, bringing hurt, pain, and devastation to innocent family members, friends, and associates as well. Sometimes people's lives are never the same after being mentally or physically abused by a predator. Let's pray together that everyone will get the professional help that they need to lead them to repentance, healing, and to the kind of peace that only God can give.

Reflecting back over the years, I can remember how I honestly felt about ministering to the very aggressive, open homosexual youth that paraded their feelings and feminine ways to staff and other youth. I did not like it and purposely did not try to minister or even waste my time talking to them.

One afternoon, I was in my office getting ready to make my rounds when the bell rang and classes let out. As I came out of my door, I noticed one youth that had on some pink, glossy lipstick on his lips that looked like make-up of some sort on his cheeks. All the boys really seemed to get excited and thrilled over him. I did not particularly like his spirit around them or me. I turned around and went right back into my office, disgusted and upset. I sat down for a while, being quiet in thought.

Afterward, though, the Holy Spirit came in and began to talk to me about serving in the ministry. He said, "What do you think I was doing when I sat with sinners and outcasts? I ate at their homes and let them know that I cared about them and loved them. I was always in their midst and walked among them. **If** you don't, how will they ever know **who I am** if they do not see it in you, son?" I was touched and felt ashamed of myself because I was taught by my parents from childhood to stay away from those who carried themselves that way. But now, I am a servant and minister of God. The Lord strengthened me and let me see my own faults.

I began to reach out to this particular young man and his crew. I started by visiting him in his housing unit, and after a while, invited him to Church and to the youth programs that I had set up with volunteers for Sunday afternoons. He began to come to Church Services. I noticed that he was really listening to the sermons. He later asked for a Bible and tracts on faith, love, and other subjects. Soon, every week, he was at Church Services and brought all of his closest peers. I began to see him tone down his aggressiveness. After that time, he never missed Church. We became friends, and I became his Chaplain. I prayed for him and his peers the same way that I prayed for all the other youth and staff. God really helped me in my weakness in that area of ministry.

After the young man had served his time, I got a letter from him about one year later. He thanked me for personally reaching out to him and showing him love without judging but being truthful through the Bible and showing him the way. He said that he was going to church and really trying to change his lifestyle, and he thanked me for introducing him to Jesus Christ. I was really moved by his letter. I remembered what the Holy Spirit had said. Now I really know and understand what serving his souls, no matter what ethnic group, race, color, or creed means. Let **all** people know that God loves them and whosoever will let him come. Praise God for His goodness, mercy, love, and grace!

...for with the LORD there is mercy, and with him is plenteous redemption.
-Psalm 130:7

17

Volunteer Programming

"...Love is greater than fear."

I started the **Grand-Parenting Mentoring** group consisting of four adults, two senior men and two senior women, recruited from the Chillicothe community. They came in twice a month and interacted with twelve youth from 6-8 p.m. every Tuesday. Social Workers were asked to select two boys from each house who they felt would benefit the most from this program. Mark, one of my Y.E.T. members, and I had initially gone to Chillicothe and met with individuals interested in working with incarcerated youth. We explained how they could help us in our quest for community volunteers, and they agreed to come!

Each session began by introducing the volunteers and explaining the program in detail to the boys. The goal was to establish a sense of stability and form positive relationships by having the youth and seniors do things together. The mentors were wise enough to know the importance of "taking time" with the young people and would just talk **and** listen to what was on their minds. They played board games and cards together and enjoyed one another's company. This arrangement was great because the grandparents loved the youth, and the youth loved them. These adults even went above and beyond the program guidelines by asking the boys to make a list of their favorite foods. I made sure that those requests were approved and the paperwork signed off. Then, the grandparents were allowed to bring in all of the homemade "goodies" specially prepared for the boys. The food was great, and the mentors always kept their promises. The program proved to be very successful. The youth who participated didn't get into trouble because they did **not** want to miss out on being with "their" grandparents!

Another program that I featured was holding **Chess Tournaments**. While making my rounds, I discovered that the majority of the boys already knew how to play chess and enjoyed it a lot. I had one volunteer, Bob, come in, and together we planned a schedule for elimination games to be held on every Unit. Bob was in charge of supervising these matches. Then, our championship game was held in the library with pictures taken of the two finalists. They received a beautiful championship certificate signed by the Superintendent, Bob, and me.

Things really started changing for the better. It was not picture perfect, but the "fear" factor was nowhere on the level that it had been before. I recruited and used volunteers to visit youth on their units. They helped and encouraged the guys with their studies and prepared those taking the G.E.D. As a result, many of the youth began going to school more. I would walk the hallways and make visits to all the classrooms several times a week.

The teachers were very responsive to my stopping by their rooms, checking on youth, and observing. My visible presence made a difference to them. Sometimes, I was asked questions by the youth and ended up telling stories about life or my travels in the ministry. The atmosphere improved greatly, and this drastic change helped to bring everyone together more than ever.

The Superintendent had frequent meetings and kept the lines of communication open. He had round-table discussions about problems and how to best deal with dangerous situations. For the **very** first time, I was asked for my counsel and put out in the forefront! Staff were afraid and wanted me, as the Chaplain, to talk and pray right then. The Superintendent even started having Departmental Head meetings twice a month instead of once a month because of the change in operating procedures and the effect the gangs were having here. Everyone got to tell what was going on in their areas and housing units, which gave me a chance to listen to problems firsthand. Then, I had an opportunity to tell everyone what my religion department was doing as well.

Continuing to focus on the needs of the youth, I was led to start an **"Adopt a House"** mentoring program. This program was designed to have positive interactions between the boys and community volunteers. After reaching out to neighborhood churches directly or through emails and word of mouth, our Y.E.T. members and I had all of those interested come in for an initial training session from 6-8:30 p.m. one evening. They were instructed on D.Y.S. rules, policies, and procedures, as well as fingerprinted, and identification pictures were taken. Further training, for going onto Units, came later after they had received background check clearance. Then, I would call them back in to receive their I.D. badges and schedules for conducting Bible Study groups.

The program proved to be very successful. Six different churches participated in this ministry so that each Unit was represented. Church teams came in on Saturday mornings from 8-10:30 a.m. once a month with usually twelve to twenty people. Each group leader had prepared his or her team ahead of time and they all knew what their exact assignments were. Several days prior to their arrival, I would go to a designated

Unit making sure to announce which church was coming and explain the program. The Officers loved that this ministry helped the youth behave because they knew that I would not let any boy participate if not on good behavior all week.

I would always notify Correction Officers, in advance, that a group was coming in on a specific day. This allowed them time to have the youth ready and seated for those morning services. The volunteers sang songs altogether, had a youth speaker, took prayer requests, and prayed. This really meant a lot to the youth because they could hardly believe, at first, that strangers they had never met, loved them so much. After services, everyone fellowshipped together playing board games, cards, chess, and holding corn hole tournaments. Then, these fun activities ended with refreshments, eating pizza, chicken wings, chips, cookies, and drinking pop!

God was working with us and answering our prayers by sending us Christian volunteers from the community not only locally but from Cleveland, Cincinnati, Dayton, Chillicothe, and Columbus. Once the new volunteers participated with their Unit and saw other needs, they asked me if they could come in and do other ministries such as give Bible studies, coaching, sports, mentoring, or tutoring. Many were allowed.

By telling the Department Head Directors what I was doing and making them aware of the Y.E.T. team's future events, helped them to see the effectiveness volunteers could have on the facility. I never had an opportunity to witness and show how prayer, caring, and unity work. These were the worst times that the institution had ever had, but I was called on by the Superintendent and God worked in our behalf. I spoke directly to this group consisting of the Nurse Supervisor, Doctor, Duty Officer, Unit Managers, Deputy Administrators, Psychologists, Psychiatrists, Cafeteria Director, School Principal, and Librarian. I said, "We have been up against great odds from the time we started back in 1993 when the facility was first constructed. We have always had to overcome unconventional circumstances to survive. In Chinese, "crisis" means "opportunity". Let's take this opportunity and make things even better than before. We do this by working together and helping each other care and communicate because what affects you affects everybody in **all** departments. Love is greater than fear."

Some Staff weren't with us from the beginning and hadn't known our history. I was asked to pray for the first time ever in a Department Head meeting. The Spirit of the Lord was with me. Staff needed encouragement because many of them had never worked with inner city youth and had never been in a dangerous environment like ours before. Those that did were still seeking support, hope, and leadership to alleviate the problems that we were constantly having every day. I knew that they needed to see courage, faith, and action. This is what they saw with less fighting in school, less man- downs on Units, and suppressed gang involvement. The positive activities being implemented by our programming for these energetic young men **was** helping and they were starting to develop better attitudes and understanding things for themselves even more. Instead of having nothing to do, which would manifest itself into trouble because an "idol" mind is the devil's workshop, they now looked forward to participating in worthwhile endeavors.

The group felt that the prayers and God had helped us when we **all** came together on one accord. Soon the whole facility asked for and welcomed volunteers in addition to wanting programs for their Units. Social Workers, who had never been in contact with me before, **now** began to email me about their troubled youth and started asking if I could put them in my programs. That's what I'm talking about! Before, they thought little of the Chaplain and the Religion Department, but **now** they realized the effectiveness and great contribution the Y.E.T. members and I had because we knew it's the foundation that upholds everything together by caring and loving each other.

The weekend was a good time to spend valuable time with the youth because they were not in school. I scheduled several programs on Saturdays where volunteers held workshops in the library to encourage them for their future. Through my Y.E.T. members and volunteers a yearly **Gospel Fest**, an all-day outdoor festival, was also planned. This event was sponsored by Mr. Grant Pedigo, Director of Mission Youth. He would always freely set up his stage and spent thousands of dollars using his very own equipment for us to operate every year without charge. All of our community Christian groups would be on the program such as: "Sons of God" Christian Motorcycle group, Chillicothe, Ohio; the All-Girls Band, Chillicothe, Ohio; "Fore Runners" Youth Band, Zanesville, Ohio; "Jesus Died for Me" Youth Mission, Columbus, Ohio; and several other Gospel Rap groups from Columbus.

During the event, tents were set up for juice, water, popcorn, and cotton candy. All of our volunteers were invited. The sun was shining brightly on a clear day, the music was lovely, and the spirit of the LORD and love spread across the grounds. What a wonderful time we all had -- Counselors, Pastors, local Church members, and family members of the youth. Those times will always be dear to me. By having this occasion outside in August with the fresh air, birds chirping, people singing, talking to one another, and laughing together made this a grand affair and especially when we didn't have any incidents. The Correction Officers loved being at work during these times also because it made their jobs fun, and they could enjoy the event activities as well.

Church Services:

On Sundays, I would come in about 8 a.m. and stay until 8 p.m. because that's when I had "free time" to minister to the boys. Sunday morning Bible classes were from 8 to 9 a.m. and Chapel Service was from 9 to 11 a.m. My volunteer Ministers conducted the Bible classes on the Units. When those classes were over, the Operations Duty Officer would make the Church call, at my request, and the Correction Officers would bring the youth over to the Gym where Services were held. We had two Officers assigned for Chapel who would stay during the entire time. The youth were required to sit with their Unit and not allowed to sit with their so called "boys".

The youth already knew my rules for Church. I had personally reviewed Church "do's and don'ts" during their religious assessment when they first arrived. Correction Officers also reminded the boys of these rules even before coming over for services because they didn't want any negative reports from me about **their** group. Then, I would reiterate this information to the guys again for anyone that was "new" or hadn't attended Church in the Gym. I told them, "This is God's time, sacred time, for these several hours. We sing, pray for our families and ourselves, and I pray for all Staff and the Institution. God's time is serious and so is mine." I had to be firm **and** loving at the same time.

They respected these procedures because this is what we did each week. We always had wonderful services that were joyful and Spirit-filled. We prayed for the Holy Spirit to always lead us and during our prayer time, many of the Correction Officers asked for special prayer along with the youth. The Holy Spirit was making all the difference on the grounds. Every day I made rounds and noticed when Staff saw me, I would always be smiling and made time when anyone wanted to talk and ask for advice, counseling, or special prayer. Everyone always told me if someone in their family was ill and even let me know about happy occasions such as birthdays, graduations, or anniversaries.

The volunteers were fantastic because they were eager, not afraid, full of the Spirit, followed the rules, and always listened to my instructions. They would go on the Units and mentor, listen, give Bible Studies, and support the youth. Their faithfulness was evident because the youth would ask me if they could participate in more activities. Many of the volunteers always came to the basketball games every year. Bob, Peg, and Kim came. Kim would always bake cookies for the team with each boy's jersey number on them.

The atmosphere was changing. Joy was replacing fear, and I knew that God was answering our prayers. However, someone in our Security Department was sending out some emails to Staff that they wanted me to either go onto the Units and conduct Church Services or get in front of a camera, with nobody in front of me, and preach, in essence, "to the walls." Certain individuals let me know about this situation, and when I prayed about it, God did not tell me to do Services that way. No one ever sent me a personal email mandating that I do this, so every Sunday morning when I came in, I continued to call for the youth, and they continued to come. I knew that the Duty Officer was uneasy about this arrangement, but his faith began to grow because he was looking at his monitor and could see and hear the Services live. No one from Operations ever called me into their office for a meeting, so I went to them to clarify things. I wanted to let them know that I knew what I was doing. The Head of Operations was off on Sundays, as well as all of the top Administrators.

The Duty Office did not really care about my duties or religious services, and when I was in Department Head meetings, where we had open discussions, comments, or complaints, no one ever said a thing about my department. I believe however that they were really afraid that the various gangs would start trouble and begin fighting. I was the one in the midst of them, and I was not afraid. I knew that it wasn't for my safety or concern but that satan was the real one behind the urgency to stop all church services and activities altogether, volunteers and all.

Well, I decided to go and see both the Deputy Administrator and the Director of Operations to talk about my church services. On this particular day and time that I went to see the Deputy Administrator, low and behold, the Director of Operations was **already** in his office! They were notably surprised to see me because I was usually never up front at the Superintendent's area unless we were having scheduled Departmental meetings. I remember being very polite but went straight to the point. I brought valid documentation for them to review from the past six weeks which, included my Sign-In sheets, Unit Sign-In sheets, and Religious Activity Sign-In sheets completed by my volunteers with the youth during that time period. These two individuals were highly impressed with this information and couldn't believe many of the names listed because some were troublesome youth or gang members. After that, they advised me to keep up the good work and good luck! Nothing was ever said about having my church services shut down again.

The youth really enjoyed and welcomed prayer. I could easily tell that many of them, especially from Cleveland, had never had prayer before or ever had anyone pray for them. This was true for most of these guys. I really knew then, the task that was ahead of me.

I delight to do thy will, O my GOD:...
-Psalm 40:8

18

Volunteer Issues

There is a way which seemeth right unto a man, but the end thereof are the ways of death.

Matthew 7:12, KJV

Now, at my job, we never had any problems with volunteers being allowed to come on grounds and go to the various housing units as scheduled. Until... around 1999, when we got a new Operations Manager. He was over security and supervised the Juvenile Correction Officers. Problems began to arise. This new Manager had transferred from the Adult Prison system and unfamiliar with the Youth system which was run totally different. As a result, there was seemingly a lack of concern, insight, or understanding as to the value and helpfulness of having volunteers interacting with the youth and the positive relationships they were forming.

My volunteers began telling me about how long they had to wait in the lobby before someone came to take them to the units. Sometimes, I was told, that they were not on the schedule **or** that they hadn't been trained, even though they had their badges pinned on to prove it!

At times, a Pastor would request to come in to see a youth from his Church. They usually had to come on a Saturday, which was my day off. So, I expressly made sure that their proper pastoral visitation papers were signed and placed in

133

the appropriate mail basket for the Operations department. However, one Monday morning, I got a call. It was from the visiting Pastor from Cleveland. He had taken his valuable time to see a particular youth because he knew that this young man would be excited someone had come to see him, especially his Pastor. The visit though was denied! He was informed by the Operations department that the "Chaplain" **did not** leave any paperwork! Some of the Secretaries on duty would tell me about these incidents as well.

Unfortunately, this dilemma occurred several more times. I was hurt and very embarrassed having to apologize and tell these devoted Pastors how sorry I was for what was happening. I reported the situation to the Superintendent and emphatically stated that if it continued, the next call would be from me to Central Office. Other Chaplains were also being confronted with similar issues. The Administration told us to put our complaints or issues in our monthly reports but from experience, we knew that these would hardly be read or considered. At our quarterly Chaplain meetings, a representative from downtown was assigned to us so that we could discuss our concerns with him directly. He, in turn, was able to report our grievances to the appropriate officials.

In 2006, everything came to fruition when the Adult Prison system started having the **same** issues! It was then that the Administration finally understood how invaluable and needed volunteers were in helping with all the predicaments prisons were facing. The Adult Prison system knew that they were about to release hundreds of inmates due to overcrowding and lack of state funds. President Bush had given the adult system eighteen million for programs to help inmates with their reentry back into society and to their respective communities. We were told by our Central Office Supervisor that the Department of Youth Services was given eight million. Personally, I did not really receive any funds to help our programs engaging our youth, neither did any of the other Chaplains.

At one of our Chaplain's meetings, each of us were told to write down what materials we needed at our respective facilities. We were told that we would **all** receive some funds for musical equipment such as keyboards or for Bibles, religious books, workbooks, choir robes, flat screen televisions, and other supplies. However, at the very next meeting, we were told that **no** funds would be coming our way! Several of the Chaplains were hoping that what we were told the **first** time would be valid, but those of us who were "veterans" really knew better because we had heard it all before. When I first started, funds were never budgeted for religious services.

So, to get back to the Adult Prison situation, the Director of Prisons along with State Officials were told by the Governor to take care of the issue. A series of Task Force meetings were held in the city for discussions with the Director of Adult Prisons, State Representative, Governor's Representative, Chaplains, Mayors, Volunteers, Pastors, and former inmates. These meetings were insightful and helpful. What eventually happened was that the Department of Adult Prison Committee wanted Chaplains to reach out to the community for volunteers to come into the prisons and help mentor, teach, and do programs to help prepare these men to be ready for society and home.

All the Chaplains were assigned dates to hold an informational assembly and mine was in December of 2006. The top officials from Central Office were present along with the Director of Youth Services, Mayor of Cir, Director of Adult Prisons, State appointed Lawyers, and State Senator of Ohio, Senator White, and Terry Collins, Director of Department of

Rehabilitation and Correction, aka DRC of Ohio. Our meeting was held in the gym and the Superintendent made it possible for every worker to attend.

Correction Officers were especially well represented because rumors were circulating that the State's financial problems could be helped by cutting their jobs and replacing them with volunteers.

When I got wind of **that** kind of thinking, it gave me some insight on why I was having problems with a few of my housing units concerning the Correction Officer mistreating my volunteers when I was not around. The meeting was excellent. The Staff had come out in full force, and I was glad to see that the Correction Officer, in question, was on the front row seat eager to ask questions.

Well, each person from Director Collins' team talked and explained what our plan entailed. As the Moderator, I gave everyone an opportunity to explain how as a team, working together, we could help make things better. I also explained the value of volunteers and had some present at the meeting. I stressed the value of these individuals who were **not** getting paid and spending **their** valuable time away from **their** families to come in and sacrifice **their** lives to help our young men who were in need!

I explained how it is to be one of the young men, incarcerated, locked up, and away from home, loved ones, and friends. In some cases, they were faced with not having families **or** their families would move and **not** let them know where they were. What made a difference? Volunteers! Volunteers can soften the blow and sometimes become the "parent" and or counselor to them. Volunteers help lessen the sadness and encourage the boys not to give up. Volunteers' reassuring words and actions also let these youth know that they **can** still make it in life to become productive citizens no matter what they've done.

In addition, I explained to the Correction Officers how these programs with the volunteers coming in to assist me were benefitting their units **and** helping them directly. Programming was one method that I was utilizing to teach the young men to be respectful, obedient, and follow the rules **or** forfeit participating in **any** of our planned functions. So, after the guys would come to any of my workshops, Bible studies, or recreational activities their characters were different because they were learning how they were to become real men.

My word was my bond, and the boys knew it. I kept my word. They knew **if** they got into trouble, they would **not** be able to come back to learn and have fun at the same time. When returning to the Units, the others who had been left behind, could see the joy on the faces of those who had participated. Their stress was gone having experienced fun **and** learning. The ones who didn't get to go could hardly believe what they heard. "You were doing what? And had what to eat?" Everyone wanted to participate then, especially the gang bangers because they didn't want to miss out on all that fun! After a while, the Staff was **always** reporting to me personally, by phone, or email **all** the youths' behavior.

In that meeting everything came together. The mayor understood and knew that these prisoners were going to be released and it would be better to help them **before** they got out because they had no education, no incentives to improve, nowhere to go, and no hope! Besides these impacting factors, the boys were scheduled to go right back to the same cities and neighborhoods that they had left. All of this was not going to be easy, but everyone understood that it was going to take everyone to come together to help make the community, family, and inmate's life better. New laws were being put before the State Court system because of **sanctions** on the inmates were still "shackles" hindering them and holding them down from being able to get work to make a decent living. Sanctions included: being unable to receive a Barber's license, even though trained; prohibiting them from getting their own shops once out; college degree programs cut; and no other rehabilitation programs initiated.

At the end we entertained questions to anyone that asked, especially the Correction Officers. I saw satisfaction on their faces when the State Representative told them emphatically that the volunteers were **not** a plan to take away their jobs. The air was cleared after that meeting. I began to see the Institution steadily begin to change.

Everyone could "see" the picture and know and feel that they were playing a part in helping the inmates' lives change for the better. A change that was better for us all.

When I retired, the last thing that I was able to tell them, was that we were **not** General Motors working with machines on an assembly line. We're working with human beings who have made mistakes in their lives and have fallen short. They could be you or someone in your family. Treat them with respect, the way you would want you or your family to be treated. We all are doing a service for God, whether you believe in Him or not. You will be held accountable.

The Chaplains had more work to do after this initial meeting and were required to meet with the Central Office Religious Program Director, Christine Money several times. We came up with a viable plan. Each Chaplain was assigned to contact seven Churches in the area and personally invite their Pastors to a Youth Summit. This event would be held at the Vineyard Church, Westerville, Ohio on September 12, 2006. A few Pastors attended but mainly volunteers and representatives from several churches. The theme was "Taking Back Our Children," a call to action for the men of faith in Central Ohio.

Malachi 4:6 states, "And He shall turn the hearts of the father to the children and the hearts of the children to their fathers." We asked them to come and hear about the opportunities to serve as mentors, tutors, coaches, program facilitators, activity and sports leaders, or consider just being a friend.

We thought it was time for Christian men to stand together to restore incarcerated and paroled youth back to the community, better equipped to be positive people when they returned home. That night I was able to bring an incarcerated youth outside of the Institution to speak about the benefits of having volunteers come and help them. The young man was from Cincinnati. He really spoke well and from his heart about the love and caring friendships that he and others had personally received by volunteers that came to the Facility each week. He said that many didn't get visits from their family members because of lack of transportation, or they lived in another city and the parents couldn't afford it. "So, to have volunteers come in to see them really means a lot because they inspire us to do better and that they really love us as well." Many Churches that were there became our partners including: New Salem Baptist, Grove City Church of the Nazarene, Bethel Temple, Central College Presbyterian, Refuge Temple, and Mt. Herman Missionary Baptist.

My help cometh from the LORD, which made heaven and earth.
-Psalm 121:2

19

Gangs

"If you can do that, you're good to go..."

O ur Institution always kept gang activity "down" and under control. However, around January 2008, a very disturbing tape recording of a riot at another youth facility got out. I didn't know anything about this incident until the Recreation Director called me into his office to see it. Usually, we would hear about trouble at our other prisons, especially something serious but were unaware of this particular facility having problems with gangs being out of control to **that** degree!

Youth were destroying their units, fighting Staff, and just going "buck wild" taking over the place. This was very disheartening for me because being the Basketball Coach and assisting the team attend both home **and** away games, I hadn't been informed of the alarming dilemma at Ma until now.

I kept the importance of this situation in the back of my mind though and would always ask how things were going on there. Unfortunately, the reports I got from a reliable source weren't good. It seemed as if that Staff was unable to control the gangs and gang leaders. The youth had destroyed ten flat screen T.V.s and the Administrators just bought them new ones. In addition, these felons were given outdoor barbecues and pizza parties to appease them! Then, not too long afterwards, in the spring, word came from the Front Office that **we** would be getting these same "gang bangers" because of finances and Ma would be closing.

Somehow, the youth at Ma found out that they were going to be shipped to Cir Correctional. Some of them had already been at our facility and had finished their treatment with us before being sent on to Ma because of their crimes. Since then, however, they had joined gangs.

So, what happened next? Cir began getting vicious, threatening emails and letters from these juvenile offenders. Staff and teachers alike were being informed of their intentions to rape and beat them down. This word spread quickly around the school and over half of the teachers quit. Fear started to take over where once there had been a more peaceful atmosphere.

I vividly remember that spring when the Ma boys first started coming in. I had never seen or felt anything like this before. The majority of these youth were Black, extremely unruly, rude, disrespectful, and the evilest acting youth that I had ever come across. Each day about five arrived or twenty-five a week, or so it seemed. The other institution was "dumping" them on us steadily and gladly saying, "good riddance!"

My job was to see and process these young men with their religious assessments quickly, which I always did. I made sure that I formally introduced myself and thoroughly explained, in detail, about Church services, counseling, Bible Study, and incoming volunteers. This bunch was very different though. Usually "new" youth would warm up to me and be glad to know that I cared and would be available to help them. Instead, these boys did not talk, always looked as if they were angry at the whole world, and never smiled. As a result, conducting assessments with them did not last as long as it did with the other youth.

Once these boys got assigned to their housing units and school, there was trouble everywhere! Teachers never closed their classroom doors because disrespectful youth were constantly disrupting their classes. Four times as many Correctional Officers were now stationed in hallways during school hours and man-down alarms (bells), that had previously gone off two or three times a day, were now ringing twelve to fifteen times on units! The gang leaders were already calling their preplanned shots to prey on any new and younger, venerable inmates.

We found out that the gangs were called the "Head-bangers" and the "Heartless" Felons. These rival gangs did not get along and, in fact, hated each other. Both groups, however, planned to outdo one another by heavily recruiting our "controlled" youth right away. They would ask a youth if he wanted some "work". Many of our guys didn't even understand, at first, what these gang members were talking about. When they would refuse, they were threatened and a "hit" put out on them from one of the gang "soldiers" who had rank. The "hit" meant that someone in the gang would sucker punch the refusing youth and try to break his jaw! The gangs also recruited by giving "join or else" ultimatums such as: taking "newbie" breakfast, lunch, and dinner meals, at times, as well as seizing their snacks on Unit before bedtime. I thought this was insane.

The "newbies" were young, so of course, could not or should not be expected to handle constant threats from gang members **bullying** them relentlessly. Dealing with incarcerated life already meant being confronted with many factors such as: being away from home and family environment, living with other guys they'd never seen before, complete strangers, with bad reputations and most of the time, much bigger. And with gangs too? They thought about "Who would protect them now?" in addition to helping them manage their own health issues, inhibitions, and fears.

A lot of the boys did not get family visits because their parents didn't have transportation and/or just could not afford it. The same was true with phone calls, most of them had to rely on letters which many never got. Their dilemma, "join the gang and supposedly get "family" support **or** constantly be threatened every day, suffering the consequences of no options was an on-going reality.

Daily life **was** hard! Imagine yourself in their shoes, even though they had committed crimes to be incarcerated, the challenges of prison were astounding. Many of the boys had issues from their upbringing or lack of it with no fathers to help raise them, brothers and sisters without help to survive, possibly mothers on drugs, tragedies in the family, or losing parents while still very young added up to a lot of pressure for these boys to deal with. And they ask themselves, "When I wake up in the morning and I see these concrete blocks every day, what do I have today to look forward to?"

The tension at the school was thick. Everyone was always on edge. All day long gang members were constantly intimidating other youth and staff. The whole atmosphere of peace changed from the time that they arrived. Their presence affected part of the normal scheduled daily activities from breakfast, lunch, and dinner to the recreation required for every unit. As a result, the Operations Department, who controlled the cameras and supervised the Correction Officers, did not let two units go to the cafeteria at the same time or fights would break out and potentially lead to dangerous rioting.

I can recall going over to the cafeteria at lunch time as usual. Operations called for one Unit to come and eat. Normally, the cafeteria would be full of one unit seated and eating while another was going through the counter line getting their food. But this time, a Correction Officer had four youth with carts getting about thirty-five "carry backs", foam containers with thirty-five individual meals, because the youth did **not** want to come over due to confrontations with other units. I had never seen anything to this degree in all of my years working for DYS and their "eating" **on** unit became a common occurrence for the next two years helping to keep trouble from taking place.

I still continued to do my daily "house" rounds, visiting a total of six units with two units per house and found that the majority of youth were there even after lunch time was over. They elected to stay locked up **on** the Unit, **in** their rooms, and **not** go to school! These youth were separated from the "new" gang members, yet fear was apparent and heavily seen everywhere. I would talk to the ones who were in their rooms. They told me that they **did** want to go to school but were getting approached by gang members asking them if they wanted some "work" meaning join their gang **or** else get "beat down". I could really understand their feelings having to go through this constantly every day. All of them stated that they would go but there was **no** control, by the Staff, to stop these out of control, predator gang members! Gang tactics decidedly caused fights to break out and led to uncalled for tension. For instance, if two gangs or individual rival members crossed paths, altercations occurred, no matter where they were.

My office was located in the school, and I think purposely put there by my friend, the principal, to be a positive influence for the boys. I can remember how hard it was for me to concentrate reading the Bible or anything else due to the tension, constant fighting, and constraints taking place. All during the morning and evenings, the man- down alarms were going off back and forth on every Unit. It was unfortunate that all the Teachers felt obligated to leave their classroom doors wide open. In this way though they could get out fast in case a fight broke out or if they had to handle an unruly youth by calling for help, whichever was the case.

For several months these situations continued and got worse. Gang members began threatening male Correctional Officers who were hired to restrain them. This deliberate resistance became very dangerous because these felons were unruly, unmanageable, and did not want to listen or follow facility rules. Instead, they had specific "numbers" and their own organized system of communicating to carry out "gang" orders.

One day these boys carried out a "hit" on C.O. "M." while he was returning to the Unit from the school and going across grounds. He was attacked by about ten youth who took his radio so that he couldn't call for help. Then, they knocked him down, kicked him, and beat him up. He got seriously injured. Luckily, however, another Correctional Officer was coming out and saw what was happening and broke it up. The injured Officer, I think, was on disability leave for about six months to a year.

Personally, I felt, that the Administration brought him back too soon or should **not** have put him back on the same Unit! If I am not mistaken, Officer M. was a veteran Marine who weighed 300 pounds or more. Even still, it didn't take long before he was attacked again by the same gang. He was hit in the head with a telephone, knocked to the ground, beaten, and kicked again!

Along with being Chaplain, I was also the Employee Assistance Program (E.A.P.) Coordinator for the Facility. My job was to let Staff know what their rights were as State employees according to State guidelines. They were entitled to receive counseling services and any other physical assistance necessary that affected their health, welfare, and ultimately their families. After meeting with Officer M. privately in my office to hear how all of these incidents had adversely affected him, it was evident that he needed **both** mental and physical support immediately. I called the downtown E.A.P. main office in his behalf, scheduled an appointment for him, and soon he got the help he needed.

Still, the same tense atmosphere persisted, and man-downs continued. It got so bad that many Staff answering "man-down" alerts were injured trying to assist on the Units. Once, I can recall going over to House Three myself to answer one of these alerts.

Running quickly from the school across grounds, almost out of breath, I arrived there with others. In no time I was able to assess the situation. The Unit was very noisy with the radio playing loudly and youth banging on their doors, wanting to get out and fight. About five Staff, by the office door, were trying to hold a youth down for attempting to attack one of the C.O.'s. The boy broke loose and ended up knocking down the Unit Manager who unfortunately was injured very badly. His leg had gotten tangled up in the scuffle and broken in three places along with his ankle. Such a loss because here was someone who truly cared about his Unit **and** the youth! Now, unable to work, he was forced to go out on disability leave for over a year. Later, when trying to return, the pressure and stress of the job proved to be just too much for him.

Things progressively continued to go from bad to worse. The majority of C.O.'s, who were really afraid of the gang members, started going out on disability and injured leave causing the First and Second shifts to be short-handed. A ripple effect occurred with the rest of the staff getting "burned-out". Mandatory overtime and working double shifts every week was exhausting. Many times, at "Roll Call", Duty Officers only had two to three employees show up. Secretaries, as well, were even working overtime, filling in for C.O.'s on Units. This situation resulted in the "faithful" staff calling off sick since they were constantly doing doubles!

In the midst of these circumstances, I soon found myself again answering another "man-down" emergency on House Three. When I got there, the majority of the youth were locked in their rooms behind steel doors. In the center of the floor, however, one belligerent youth was arguing with the Correction Officer in charge and unwilling to cooperate. Then, another boy came from upstairs who was refusing to go into his room as well. Things began to heat up even more between the quarreling youth and the Officer. He intentionally kept challenging the C.O., not caring about his commands or Unit authority, and began cursing. The Officer, in turn, was starting to lose his patience while this boy continued trying to "get" to him. Meanwhile, more Officers arrived and demanded that the youth who had come downstairs go to his room immediately. When defiantly refusing to do so, he got "escorted", meaning that they were justified to use "hands on" to help him go in the right direction.

Ordinarily, when I would come on the scene, things would usually start to calm down just because of my presence, even though the gang members didn't know me that well. Suddenly, however, when the inmates, who were already locked up, saw their gang member being "handled" and manually taken to his room, they began making loud noises, cursing, threatening staff, and beating on their doors for what seemed like five to ten minutes straight. It got so loud that you could hardly think. The spirit at that moment changed in the House, becoming demonic and evil all at once. Boom! Boom! Boom! "Come get some of this!" a youth angrily challenged an adult. I didn't have time to step in. Everything was happening so fast and escalating very quickly. Boom! Boom!

Bolts began loosening from the wall and before I knew it, the cell doors came open from the youth constantly kicking them and screaming about dying with their gang family. I looked in their faces and they appeared to be in some type of evil trance. One at a time, doors were knocked open, and they were about to come out with fire in their eyes, screaming that they were going to kill and mess up everything in the House! Out of all my years in DYS, I had never been in a scene like this. There was truly a demonic frenzy in that House!

It was the very first time that fear came over me, not that I was afraid for myself, but I was afraid for the Staff and what could happen -- blood, broken bones, teeth knocked out, someone paralyzed. I remember stepping towards the middle of the Unit, in the crowd, briefly closing my eyes and calling on God to help us. I kept saying, "Jesus, Jesus, Jesus, we need **You** now!" The youth did not come out of their rooms after kicking the doors open. It was as if an angel stood in front of them. I began to go door to door just looking at each youth while they were calming down and the noise started dying down. I stared at them and told them, "No need to come out." "You good?" "Good." All the Staff started slowly shutting the doors back, but they could not lock them because they were broken. This incident was very intense and stressful to say the least. Unfortunately, I had **already** witnessed scenes of blood, broken bones, and injuries all before that warranted the services of an Emergency Squad and follow up visits from me to see the injured parties, **both** individual youth and Staff at the hospital.

Later, I went to my office and began to pray. At Church, I had repeatedly stressed to the boys always P.U.S.H. "Pray Until Something Happens." Much prayer, much power.

Little prayer, little power. No prayer, no power. God will hear you when you call and will answer your prayers. I began to pray over the situation and ask God what to do and how could I help with this evil gang situation effecting the whole Institution. It was Mother's Day afternoon when God answered my prayers. He told me to go seek out the gang leaders and talk to them. I did not know who they were, but I had heard rumors that they stayed on House Three. This House had had **all** the "man-downs" and was where most of the trouble was taking place. I asked some of the boys that I could trust to tell me who the leaders were and got their names.

I called the Unit, and the C.O. was happy to let me know that she had both of the youth that I had asked for. She said that both of them were sitting there watching television. I told her that I would be right over to visit with them. She said, "Anytime. Thank you, Chap very much." Usually, an entire Unit is out together watching shows, but it seemed that the C.O.'s wanted to keep these two "kingpins" separated from everyone else. So, they were the only ones watching the T.V. right then. All the others were locked up in their rooms.

I came on Unit and stepped in front of the television. I introduced myself and said that I would like a few minutes to talk to them. Then, I cut the T.V. off and walked past them with my back turned and went to a table where we could sit down. When I turned around, they were right behind me, and we sat down together. I knew that I had God on my side and that these young men, nineteen and twenty, were not as wise and didn't know more about life than me. A few minutes turned into four hours. I started off by asking them did they know what day it was. The second in command seemed puzzled but the leader said that it was "Mother's Day" today and that's how I began starting our relationship and dialogue. I talked about how their mothers had carried them for nine months and probably raised them to make something out of their lives, but now, I asked, "you reward them by becoming incarcerated in a state facility?"

As our conversation continued, I talked to them and gave them a brighter picture about the beautiful things God has given us in this world. Things taken for granted such as: the trees, grass, the rivers and oceans, family, and true friends. I told them about what's in the ocean world, scuba diving, snorkeling, going on a cruise ship for a week or two, and how great, exciting, and fun it actually is. I began to open up their minds and let them dream a while. I asked them had they ever been out west to Texas or maybe Arizona to see and ride the beautiful horses of the wild west. Did they ever go to the Grand Canyon or visit the other wonders of the world? I told them how they had everything in them to make all these things come true in their lives. A brain, use it correctly, make the right decisions. Education, listening, and learning is the key. It's never too late! All attainable choices.

They both had ambitions. I let them talk but I don't recall what they wanted to be. I do remember, however, that we shook hands and that they had forgotten all about the movie that they were previously looking at. They were thankful that I came to see them. The other youth and gang members could not believe what had just happened. No cursing. No hollering. No disturbance at all. Just a peaceful Sunday afternoon.

Later on, I reviewed my files to see if I had ever given these two young men an interview assessment because my practice was to do that to every youth that came into the Facility. Indeed, I had. I checked my papers and discovered that the leader was from Cleveland, Ohio and had put down for his religion that he was a Seventh-day Adventist. The majority of the time, the youth would put down what their parents are, and they would make the same claim.

I told the two gang leaders that I would be checking in on them from time to time. So, the next week, I purposely made time to see the Number One leader. Both of the leaders though were still on the same Unit at that particular time, and both were considered too dangerous to be let out of their rooms. They were on mandatory "twenty-four-hour lock down" because of past occurrences pending from their previous facility but were still allowed out for one hour at Cir. Because of my Chaplain status, I had special privileges to see any youth who were on "lock down" and a master key to let myself into their rooms after notifying the Correction Officer on duty and signing in on the "Sign In" form. Most youth looked forward to such visits from someone who cares and that they could trust.

The main leader was surprised to see me. We talked for several hours, just about himself and his family. I let him know that I knew about the Seventh-day Adventist religion because I was one. He told me that his grandmother took him all the time when he was a young kid. He did know what she practiced but he stopped going when he got older. I knew that the "kingpin," what they would also call themselves, was really welcoming my visit because he was not allowed to mix with or have any contact with the other youth on the Unit.

When I would begin to leave, I knew that the other boys were always watching and wondering what was going on. I also understood that they respected and operated with certain standards in mind: authority, respect, power, and fear. They knew that I was a man of God and saw three of those same standards reflected in me. I did not fear them however and never showed fear at any time. If there was to be any "fear", **God** said, "Let them **fear Me**, because **I** am greater than satan and evil"! I asked the "kingpin" if he wanted me to come back and he said, "Yes." He enjoyed talking to me. I realized that he got lonesome and that I was a lifeline to what was going on around grounds for him, even though his peers invariably came up with ways to communicate with him despite lock down.

I do remember telling this "Kingpin" that he needed to turn his life around so there would be a future for him instead of prison. He told me that he was not putting out the call for hits on youth or staff. I said to him that these things were taking place and **if** you are the "kingpin" none of these things would be happening **if** you indeed have the power. I gave him a lot to think about as I tried to get him to choose his power to make things better, in a positive way, for the younger generation who were watching and following his example. About a week later though, he got transferred to another facility. I really wished that I had had more time to work with him.

Well, not too long after the main leader was gone, the Number Two leader was shipped out as well. Central Office supposedly was separating the two youth, hoping to break up their power and leadership. That was a start, but I always felt that it was just like putting a band-aid on the whole gang problem. Soon after the two leaders were gone, others in rank began stepping up through the ranks and seemingly took over, calling the shots during the gang's second month at Cir. The Highway Patrol SWAT Team was also called in. They had to ship out several vicious and extremely dangerous gang members who repeatedly refused instruction from anyone. These guys chose to be invariably violent and whenever allowed out of their rooms, constantly threatened Staff and fought other youth who refused to join them. Their attacks were so violent that they got "bound over" to adult prison.

Soon after these incidents, gang activity decreased but not entirely. I think that the gang youth had to reorganize and see who their real leaders actually were now. Even though the atmosphere was not peaceful, it was not as bad as before. There was still not much movement on or across the grounds. No school activities, indoor or supervised outdoor rec, or even going to the cafeteria! Second shift Correction Officers, starting at 2 p.m., would usually supervise outside rec such as basketball, football, or just getting some fresh air for any youth not in school and after count had been taken. However, none of these activities were taking place because the boys refused to go to **anything**! Sometimes just two or three youth were brought to the gym but for the most part, an Officer would call the Rec Department and cancel. This went on for weeks and months which was ridiculous! Everybody was letting fear set in and caused them to shut down everything.

Church - Afternoon Programs

By this time, more of the gang members had seen me all over the grounds and they knew that I was the Chaplain, aka "Chap". The only activities that continued and ongoing were Church related. These were ones that I had planned and implemented, including Sunday morning Church Services, Tuesday evening workshops with twelve to fifteen youth, and Sunday movie times. Then, every other Sunday afternoon I scheduled a special Youth Church program. A guest Pastor would be invited to bring his Church and conduct the afternoon program from 1 to 3:30 p.m. with youth speakers, singers, and testimonies from their younger and older members.

We would meet in the library, and I would have the area prearranged with seating for thirty to forty of my youth. The special guests were always seated behind my pulpit and kept separate from the young men during Services. However, after singing, praying, and hearing the sermon, I allowed the guests to mingle with my boys. I gave everyone a questionnaire asking them to find someone who each answer applied to and have them initial it. For instance, "Who has a birthday in December?" or "Who's favorite color is red?" or "Who was born in July?" The youth were ecstatic as well as the Church guests. They loved the activity and both sides became more relaxed, smiling and laughing, while meeting and greeting each other playing the game.

This occasion happened to be the very first time for one Pastor and his congregation to come. He had been deeply interested in Prison Ministry and reached out to me concerning how his Church could be of service. I met with him and his wife at the Institution and took them on a tour of the entire grounds. He had already spoken with his members about going outside of their church to do this ministry and they were willing to be used by God. I gave the couple training prior to scheduling our date so that they were well aware of exactly how everything would proceed. And now, their first time coming was here! I prayed for them when they arrived because I could see some nervousness.

After the "Icebreaker," we separated everyone into teams and played another game called **"Bible Football."** Each side was able to choose their own players until they had fifteen participants apiece. One by one, individual players were asked a question in order to score points for their respective teams. We had yardage markers just like a regular football field -- 5, 10, 20, and so forth plus a real football to place and move every time someone got the answer right. There were even "extra" point questions given for knowing popular teen-related trivia as well as penalties if the rules were broken.

When we finished playing the games, it was time to eat! The Church had brought in food for everyone. Pizzas, chicken wings, chips, and pop! We all ate together and really had true Christian fun and fellowship. My youth had had the time of their lives! They hated to leave when time was up.

Shortly after they had gone, I received a phone call from the Pastor on his way back to Groveport, Ohio. Only a half hour had gone by! But he couldn't wait any longer and wanted me to know how the services had impacted and affected his members, his wife, and himself. He and his wife were crying and elated over the great time that they all had had and how his members couldn't stop talking about it! The very next week, he contacted me again asking if his group could come once a month. His entire Church by now had heard about the wonderful experience and wanted to be included. So, we continued to do just that every month!

There's nothing better than when the youth **themselves** tell others, back on Unit, about "all" the fun they were having! I didn't have to ask for more participants. Gang members even wanted to come and began asking me why I did not call them over. I explained that they were welcome **but** that they had to follow **all** of my rules to participate, which meant, no fighting, cursing, being respectful to my guests and myself, and to appreciate the program because it was planned especially for them. "**If** you can do that, you're good to go. I will sign you up next time." So, I did. These guys never broke their promises, and I never had a fight or any trouble out of any of them!

Extra Activities

Now, getting back to the atmosphere on grounds, as I mentioned before, besides my activities, everything else was stagnant. There was little or no daily scheduled recreation for the whole grounds and the Correction Officers were no longer bringing the youth out during the afternoon or evening for recreation like they were accustomed to doing. I thought this was crazy!

Following the Lord's leading, I decided that enough was enough and something had to be done. I went to the Recreation Director and asked for the touch football flags and shirts so I could get a game going on the football field. He informed me that Mr. "Woo Woo", our nickname for him, and the Head of Operations, had taken all the football equipment. Everything was locked up and anyone who wanted to use it had to get permission from his office. No problem. I went and asked for the equipment. The officer on duty was kind of shocked when I told him what I was planning to do with the gang youth from the worst two units at the facility. I signed for the equipment, took it to my office, then called Houses, Maple, and Hickory, to play each other. I talked to Mr. W., an exceptional Social Worker, who knew how to talk to the youth and visibly respected by them to help me. He was excited about the idea of a football challenge.

I got him to ask the guys who would be interested in playing and have them sign up on the Sign-In Sheet. He also let them know that I would be down to talk to them personally about the rules, **my rules**, that would apply, and I went by. The same agreement went for both Units. A half hour later, I went and talked to the Maple and then Hickory boys. Both Units gave me their word, **one youth at a time**, that they would **not** cause any trouble. I said, "Okay." Then, I went out the front door and had them follow me single file to the field, along with Mr. W. Next, I got those from Maple and came out the same way, single file. After we explained the football rules again, Mr. W. and I refereed.

The youth were ecstatic about being outside, getting fresh air, and being able to compete on the football field. Remember now, that these were two "rival" gangs that **hated** one another. They had put their differences aside though because they were getting a chance to play sports and let me see their athletic abilities. The game was close. I think the team that won only won by an extra point. The score ended up in the forties when time ran out. Both sides played hard. I had them line up and shake hands when we finished. They did. Everyone was happy and wanted to know **if** they could play again the next day.

That day was the beginning of positive change for the whole institution. Mr. W. and I continued to work with both housing units playing sports, not only football, but conducted basketball tournaments, and held track meets in the afternoons following dinner. All the other Units began hearing about everything we were doing and eventually saw us for themselves outside having fun. They wanted to participate too and soon fear was replaced by a less defensive attitude that said maybe, let's try this out and see.

After a while, the boys' desire to be involved picked up even more and the Units started doing recreational activities again under controlled rules and environment. We ended up having flag football tournaments for the entire facility. The teams were given jerseys and were allowed to use face paint just like the pros. All the Unit Managers and Social Workers got involved and came out to support their housing units. Games were scheduled in the mornings and evenings. The Recreation Department prepare the field with yard stripes marked off and we had licensed staff referees who made sure all calls were in accordance with league regulations. I also made sure that I had little pep talks and prayer with the players before each game. God blessed us throughout the season **without** any incidents!

I took group pictures of the teams and got permission to put them up in the hallways of the school. The boys loved seeing themselves in a positive light like that. The principal pledged to put a large picture of the team that won the championship in his office to show his support as well. All of these events led up to opening the door for additional programming at the institution. The Operations Office finally began to trust and see that we **could** do things **if** they were planned and well supervised.

Let thy mercy, O LORD, be upon us according as we hope in thee.
-Psalm 33:27

Receiving New Youth

L et me share with you this story from The Columbus Dispatch newspaper quote, *"Marion, Ohio - Twice in 90 minutes Juvenile Correction Officers ran across the massive courtyard in response to man-down alarms, calls by other guards seeking help."* *The electronic pleas for assistance constituted business as usual on a recent afternoon in the Marion Juvenile Correction facility. Another fight. Another unruly youth. Another act of violence. Another day at Marion. The home to 294 of Ohio's oldest and worst juvenile offenders is out of control amid violent assaults, gang activity and a shortage of guards, critics suggest. The numbers last year 316 youth on youth assaults and 188 youth on Staff assaults escalated by a third from 2006. It is a place, state officials agree, that must change to avoid being little more than a teenage way station on the path to more crime and adult time. About 1,700 Department of Youth Services and State Highway Patrol incident reports from 2007 and hundreds of pages of expert findings form a common bottom line. 'Marion is a dangerous place'* one fact finder named Fred Cohen wrote.

He was a Law Professor, called upon to examine six state correction systems, as well as other specialists, examined Ohio's juvenile facilities as part of a pending lawsuit to improve conditions. Their findings and a Dispatch review of State records demonstrated the depth of Marion's problems. The article continued, *"Outnumbered, overworked, and undertrained juvenile Correctional Officers are afraid of the boys. Half of those confined are adults doing time for violent crimes. Youths can*

161

be held in youth services institutions until age 21. Assaults on Staff members occurred such as bites, blown-out knees, and the indignity of being doused with milk cartons filled with urine.

Guards, teachers, and other prison workers regularly are assaulted. Last year, they missed the equivalent of seven years of workdays because of injuries and disabilities. Large youth fights have sent Staff to the hospital four, five, and six at a time. Slightly more than half of the frustrated, frightened, and fatigued guards quit last year in 2007, some walking away from $15.80 an hour jobs only after a few days. More than a third of the prisoners are Heartless Felons or Head Busters, feuding gangs, that control contraband and demand 'taxes' on food and hygiene items. Members of the Felons, the dominant gang, are from Cleveland, Youngstown, and Toledo. The Head Busters are from Cincinnati, Dayton, and Columbus."

"It will be a huge challenge to turn Marion around," said Alphonse Gerhardstein, a Cincinnati Lawyer handling the settlement of the youth-services lawsuit on behalf of youth and their families. *"It's in crisis and everyone knows it. The violence must be addressed."*

"Dion Norman, the Superintendent at Marion said *the department officials for the first time are 'sending a message' to the gangs and "wanna be" gangsters. On January 24, 2008, the flashing of gang signs over breakfast led to a disturbance that nearly turned into a riot. More than 100 inmates ran loose in the cafeteria and courtyard fighting for several minutes. Marion sent out an emergency call for assistance from State Troopers.*

One Union leader was very alarmed and said the ratio of youth to guards are twelve to one on the grounds and twenty-four to one in the Unit housing. In the use of Ohio's gang law in a juvenile facility, State Officials are seeking indictments to charge as many as two dozen inmates with participating in a criminal gang in hopes of packing them off to adult prisons. 'A small amount of kids cause most of the problems', Norman said.

These are, he said, *'tough older, bigger kids from broken homes with little education and little hope. They are tough to turn around. All the courts do when they send them to us is take the guns out of their hands. We're winning the battle; we need more resources.' The department recently announced that it's moving to release up to 200 of 1,800 statewide offenders near the end of their terms."*

The solution to Ma problem was **not** rectified in the manner alluded to in the article and **did not** move the facility. Instead, officials "moved" the youth! A decision came down from them quickly to close the Ma Institution after first opening its doors in 1999.

Problems and all, Ma's worst youth, were just transferred **to us** at Cir! Now, I was confronted with **their** issues! However, I was blessed to have approximately one hundred twenty-five volunteers that we had already trained and processed in-house. They were eager and active to serve and came from all parts of Ohio such as: Cleveland, Columbus, Akron, Cincinnati, Springfield, Dayton, and Grove City.

I had two of them speak at our annual Volunteer Banquet. One was a Staff member from our Y.E.T. Team and the other was my "fireball," my nickname for her, a volunteer named P. She spoke on God's chosen people, Israel, and how God always helped them **when** they obeyed Him. She was referring to what happened at "Jericho" in this instance and how a seemingly impossible situation was made possible **with** God. Out of her presentation, we were led to let God use us in the same manner. The Holy Spirit impressed our group to "march" around the grounds seven times for the gang problem that had been passed on to us. Our job was to believe that

God would once again take a seemingly impossible situation and work it out in our behalf.

We organized with these two ladies and had Lucinda taking charge of getting specific prayer requests from each Department which included: Administration - Superintendent and Staff, Human Resources, Operations - Control, Lobby, and Guard Shack employees, School Personnel - Principal and Teachers, Recreation, Food Service, Mental & Physical Health Workers - Psychologists, Social Workers, and Medical, Maintenance, Storeroom, Unit Managers, Supervisors, as well as Houses One, Two, and Three. Their requests were definitely sincere asking for peace, security, safe working environment, guidance, healing from sickness, positive youth change, personal and family needs.

After several meetings, we scheduled our **"Jericho" march** for one Sunday afternoon in May 2009 at 2 p.m. We met with about thirty brave, Christian volunteers, prayer warriors, both men and women, in the school library. After I gave a brief sermonette, we had prayer, sang one song, and then I gave instructions on how we would proceed as a unified group marching around all the Units. The Facility was designed with buildings on both sides of the grounds. The Cafeteria, School, and Warehouse were on the right and three side-by-side Housing Units on the left. In the middle was a grassy, courtyard area with a black-topped track enclosing it in front of the buildings.

The boys were inside looking out of their small windows in shock. Not knowing what was going on, they saw me in front and many of them were trying to get my attention with their hands and mouths moving with puzzled faces. I did not stop to answer them. I only motioned back with praying hands. We kept marching all around the grounds six times while seriously praying with the prayer requests in our hands. Each volunteer had been assigned to pray for a specific Department and did so as we continued to march slowly around the track. We all could feel the power of the Holy Ghost as we took each step. What an exciting moment!

It seemed like the youth began telling others and soon more of them were looking out the windows at us, as we kept on marching and praying in faith that God would hear us and answer our prayers. None of the youth watching were vulgar. They just watched in amazement. On the seventh and last time around, we sang and shouted as we went and eventually stopped in front of the school where we had begun. We circled up and I had everyone lock arms like a chain and closed with prayer. Then, we all parted with joy and happiness for serving God at the facility.

I felt genuinely proud to be in that position being a Seventh-day Adventist Chaplain. The very next day, several of the youth saw me making my rounds. They began asking about Sunday afternoon. Many said that they saw us. They were sincerely impressed by the fact that we were **really** praying for them. These inner-city gang members, who I knew, could **not** believe what they had witnessed and told me what it meant to them! Usually acting as if nothing bothered them was and had always been their "front", their facade, because they didn't think people honestly cared about them **that** way; enough to come in and pray for them **and** their families. Seeing the volunteer "marchers" made a difference.

God **was** moving as we were praying. Change **did** come! Positive change with less stress and less man-downs. The school became calmer, and you could see the teachers becoming more relaxed and able to teach again. Movement on grounds came back and groups started going to the cafeteria for their meals instead of ordering carry backs every day. I knew that God was working in our behalf. Units were attending scheduled "Rec" again and things continued moving in the right direction. Surprisingly, Social Workers even started emailing me about scheduled events and keeping me abreast of individual boys that needed help with schoolwork or counseling. This was great! Departments were increasingly working hand-in-hand with regular meetings, talking and giving advice, as well as communicating positive or negative feedback.

Things **do** come together when everyone gets on the same page, not being isolated or selfish, and choose to help one another! Just like when Christ ascended back to Heaven, the disciples were in disarray arguing, afraid, and discontent. But it was only at Pentecost, when they got on one accord, did change happen. Then, the Holy Spirit came down and blessed them with power to do God's work. It's when we **trust and obey** that God will keep His promise and **always** show up and show out!

I was happy to see the facility become alive again. The volunteers were appreciated instead of being considered a "burden". Each Unit Manager didn't want his House to be left out of any activities going on because they finally realized the benefit of having volunteers. They especially saw the positive effect these dedicated Christians had had on the youth **and** Staff. Workers even started feeling comfortable enough with me to share how various ministries were being conducted at their own Churches and how their members wanted to come and volunteer as well.

Every day you could see things changing for the better. Many of the youth who were previously afraid to go to school were now in attendance and the number of students increased. I had volunteers V., P., and K., "The Three Amigos", help the young men with schoolwork. They taught those who could not read and encouraged them to keep on going to school and get an education. Every week these dedicated women came three to four days, staying four to five hours and sometimes twice in one day, when needed! God answered my prayer by sending these Christian warriors to help me. I could never have been able to handle all of these things by myself. Most of all, I was grateful to see that the Institution began to recognize volunteers as productive, helpful, valuable individuals, and **never** a threat to take away anyone's job.

Wait on the LORD: be of good courage, and he shall strengthen thine heart...
-Psalm 27:14

Dealing with Situational Problems

Most of the time it took listening and communication skills to solve many of the problems that occurred.

I have always said that the Department has "professional" positions but **not** necessarily people who are professionals. I can recall times when I was at work and while checking my emails read about numerous problems happening on Units. For instance, one youth from the mentally challenged Unit was placed on an isolation restriction. Allegedly he had found a sharp object and stuck it in his mouth; refusing to return it. In order not to harm himself, he was put into a "flight" jacket and stripped of all his clothing. These necessary precautions were the correct measures to take at the time.

After I found out and a week went by, I noticed that this boy was missing from Church. He usually attended and now I had not seen him. So, I decided to go and check for myself what the problem and fuss was all about. He was in the Isolation Room, and I went to the door. It was about noontime and since his Unit was gone to lunch, I didn't have any interference with other guys trying to make him upset. I said, "K., where have you been?" As I spoke to him, we were both smiling.

I told him that I had written him a ticket, a "Church" ticket, just like Police Officers give when drivers break the law for speeding or something. I showed it to him, and he laughed a lot. I had made small pieces of paper into little tickets that said, "Faith Chapel Church Services". I missed you this week!" signed Chaplain Benton and I had the person's name on it that was absent. He was ecstatic! He said, "I won't miss anymore." I said, "If you do, I will be looking for you!" Then I said, "What are you doing in that new suit?" I already knew. He looked down.

Next, I asked him what was in his mouth which he readily opened and showed me. After that, I asked him to give it to me. As I unlocked the door, he gave me the small piece of plastic, about one inch long, quite easily, just like that! This interaction only took about four minutes. He got released the same evening after I informed the Psychologist and Psychiatrist. Most of the time it took listening and communication skills to solve many of the problems that occurred. Rumors had spread all week long that he had had a razor blade under his tongue which was totally untrue. The Correction Officers, however, were relieved and everyone was glad that he was sent back to his own room and could now join in with his Unit's activities.

Another incident occurred in 2001, when common sense was not used again. This time a different youth off of the high risk, mentally challenged Unit, broke from the line going to dinner. He ran around the housing building, climbed onto the roof, and refused to come down. All available Staff were called. I can remember it so plainly because I was on my way to clock out that day. I stopped again to see what the problem was.

The young man was very angry and screaming out that he would jump if anyone tried to come up and get him. The Superintendent, Deputy Assistant, Director of Operations, and other top Administrators were trying to talk him down, yet their attempts seemed only to upset him more. Eventually, they gave up trying to reason with the youth and went back to their respective offices. I waited until they were done before approaching the situation. I knew this kid pretty well because at one time he was in one of my gospel choirs. I began talking calmly to him and asked what was bothering him. He told me that the Correction Officer on Unit took his "championship" belt. I knew something had to have set him off like that because he was usually a joyful and happy young man.

This youth had a belt that he had gotten permission to make because I was over at the gym when he made it and the Recreation Director showed it to me. "E." was very proud of his belt because he had made it himself from pieces cut out of a cardboard box.

I told him that I would take care of the problem and make sure to talk to the Officer. I also assured him that this dilemma would be resolved quickly and see if he could have his belt back. He said, "OK, but don't go home Chap because after you leave, they will not let me have my shower and I won't get to eat." I said, "Is that right? Don't worry. You can trust me." He came down and we both walked back to his housing Unit together. The Correction Officer and I talked everything over and made an agreement. No problem. I asked that his belt be returned to him the next day.

As I was leaving, I stopped to touch base with the Director of Operations, Mr. M., who happened to be talking with my Supervisor and the Finance Administrator. They were discussing the incident when I overheard the Director of Operations say that this youth was **not** going to eat **or** get a shower. Just what the youth had said! I was shocked. I said, "Not while I'm here." I stayed two extra hours to take care of this predicament since I gave my word. I said, "Yes, he **will** get to shower if I have to go over and supervise it myself." I informed all three of these men that that's why we have training for just these types of situations.

The mentally challenged youth are very sensitive and easily upset. So, that's when our verbal skills are to come into play, not to bully them or not show compassion. They always understand when someone talks to them with thoughtfulness and care. The Officials had all agreed with the Operations Director **until** I made a stand and refuted what he said. I then marched back to the Unit, got the boy a hot meal, and waited until he came out of the shower and put it into his room for the night. He **and** the Correction Officer smiled. The youth because his needs were met, and the Officer because his Unit would have a quiet night now since the rest of the youth had seen everything firsthand.

Some other issues surfaced directly from the Operations Department after a "new" person was hired from the adult prison system. He took over for the recently retired Director of thirty years. Up to this time, I had had **no** difficulties whatsoever with paperwork being handled in a timely manner from them. Operations was in charge of transportation on and off grounds as well as all security. It consisted of a Director plus JCOs supervised by him. Ordinarily, when a youth had a death of a parent or close family member, transportation was provided to go to the funeral viewing or hospital visitation as long as I accompanied him there. However, **if** a JCO didn't care for a certain youth, he would purposely leave the paperwork requesting transportation on his desk indefinitely. His actions hindered the procedural process so that adequate staff couldn't be available. When this spiteful nonsense started happening to me, I went right up front and let them know that I would continue to go on every funeral viewing **personally** as well as the hospital visitations allowed for these young men when sickness or death occurred. I was determined **not** to let them be denied seeing their loved ones solely because Operations did not care. So, all the while at **Cir**, I continued taking boys in spite of opposition to Cleveland, Cincinnati, Springfield, Dayton, Columbus, and other small counties in Ohio whenever necessary. I was well aware that giving consideration in this regard did not matter to various people in leadership positions, but really understood that satan was behind all of these hindrances facing me. I also knew though that **God** was on my side helping in times of need in **every** situation that I encountered. After I prayed, **God** would **always** work things out for good!

Over my entire career, I've observed so many times where situations have gone awry. How different could've been the outcomes **if** only verbal skills and "cool" heads had prevailed. Repeatedly, Correction Officers made serious errors by choosing to use material things or activities as options to withhold from the boys. These items were considered "pay back" by them because **they** failed to control their youth on the Units; whether a phone call home, movie night with "Chap", basketball games, or even Church Services. I constantly had to educate Staff in this area because I was **not** going to allow them to punish a youth using **my** programs as leverage. If a young man did do something wrong, he had a right to a hearing and until then, he would be free to participate, especially for Church Services! The goal was to build the boys **up**, not continue to tear them down! For you see, the same youth that Staff labeled as "bad" and "troublemakers", were the same ones that I didn't have any problems with because I saw their needs **not** behavior; **real** human beings inside who only needed someone to really care.

In addition to performing my Chaplaincy duties, I became the Coach and Assistant Coach for the basketball team over several years. Here was another example of when Staff tried to use forfeiting playing as a reprimand for some of our players. Every time it was game time, mostly the day before, we would get an email from someone on Staff stating that one of our team's players was **not** going to play! They failed to see that our program was designed to help engage the youth in positive ways as well as lessen fighting and gang activity. Our adult Coaching Staff had even held meetings with all the other DYS Institutions. Together, we voted to have basketball try-outs and eventually uniformed teams playing during the official basketball season, using the same rules as the Ohio High School Basketball Association. We did just that!

These boys were trained and really enjoyed playing. But, like I said, our own Staff, from the Units, wanted to **punish** youth **instead of teaching** them. We would ask what had these players done wrong and usually it didn't call for them to miss a game. I told Staff in meetings that it was not up to them to make these decisions. "We" were their Coaches and felt that "we" should make these types of disciplinary calls. So, we did! If players did not make the grade, they were ineligible. They had to go to school, get passing grades, and be respectful to Staff as well as to other youth. When that did not happen, "we," their Coaches, would vote on which discipline or suspension to use. Some Staff still did not take time to see or care about how much time we had invested in working with the boys.

One of the Coaches sacrificed his time and came in two hours early **before** his regular shift started to have practice with the boys. He did not get paid for that, yet he did it because he cared. Additionally, our away games were in the evenings, after dinner, and usually started around 6:30 p.m. Sometimes, we would not get back from Cleveland until about 11 p.m. It didn't matter to us that we weren't getting paid for the extra hours past our regular check out time. We loved what we were doing, teaching the young guys about life through basketball. I always said that there is no "I" in TEAM. "Being on this team is hard work, just like life. No man is an island. Everyone needs someone else in life to make it with discipline, determination, resilience, mental toughness, loyalty, accountability, and unity." We stressed all these things for two weeks before they even saw a basketball! They were upset at first, but as time went by, they began to learn the true meanings of these words and became better on the court. I told them that they would always have two qualities that we were giving them to carry on in life. First, "Don't quit no matter what the score is" and that's how they learned to play and second, "when you get knocked down seven times, the Bible says get up eight!"

In God is my salvation and my glory: the rock of my strength, and my refuge, is in God.
-Psalm 62:7

Long Term Programs

*Every day it was wonderful to witness the Holy Spirit
working on their hardened hearts and eventually see them
break down and allow the love that was penetrating their
hearts to take command.*

E ven though everything was not all "peaches and
cream", we got back to our regular routine and
became once again one of the best, if not "the best",
existing Department of Youth Services Institution still in oper-
ation. The most violent boys noticed how different we were
from Ma. They observed the other youth having fun and being
happy, so they too began to respond more positively. I started
choosing several gang young men to be involved in my Christian groups that had programs lasting for six months. **Kairos
Torch** was one and **Epiphany** was the other.

Kairos is a select group of volunteers and members from
local Churches, the U.S., and the world dedicated to being mentors for incarcerated youth. Their program is very well organized, and each volunteer agrees to work with his assigned
young person for the specified six-month time period. They
focus on boys developing their own reasoning abilities to help
them make better decisions in life.

The starting weekend consists of three days with the thirty
pre-selected youth being engaged all day. Initially, they are

asked to join a table with other volunteers and then make up their "table" family name. Many of the boys learned to look on the inside of themselves and understand who they really are for the first time. They got to hear true life stories given by the adults and participated themselves by sharing their artwork made during sessions. These interactive activities helped them learn to forgive others as well as learn how to let go of abusive things that had happened to them.

I felt blessed and excited when it was time for Kairos Torch to come because they had such an impressive impact on our grounds spreading joy and love through their prayers and fellowship. We were **all** very glad to have them. In fact, our institution became the very first juvenile facility to have this type of program in Ohio. And from day one, not only with their prayers and fellowship, but also with their generosity and kindness, the Kairos Torch team had an unforgettable presence! They would bring **every** employee and **every** youth in the whole institution a dozen home-baked cookies made especially for everyone by the grandmothers of Kairos! Coconut, chocolate chip, oatmeal, peanut butter, and just about every other kind of mouth-watering, super-sized assortment was baked with love and genuinely tasted in every bite! These were a **big** hit on Campus.

Also, during one of the sessions, each youth was given a birthday cake with their name on it. Many of these guys had never experienced having a birthday party or cake before and it meant a lot to them. Since we stayed together for eight hours of the day, our lunches and dinners were provided by the group. These meals were always prepared by their own members and brought into the facility; hot, delicious, and ready to eat.

Personally, I thoroughly enjoyed being involved supervising and participating in the program. On the last day, the youth are marched down to the gym for graduation. They now surprisingly meet their "new" Christian family that we had come in without them knowing it. These individuals give the youth a welcoming, standing ovation. The youth are shocked and extremely overjoyed to find out about this "new" life in Christ that **they** can have. After the ovation and singing, each "table" family is introduced. Then, each youth tells what he has learned and how he's enjoyed being selected for this outstanding event. Finally, at the very end, the entire Kairos team is introduced, including the cooks from the community, truck drivers who delivered the food, and those who contributed funds to help make everything possible. Even following the concluding graduation, twenty Kairos team members continued coming in every Monday mentoring their assigned youth for six months.

After Kairos Torch, I scheduled another similar group, Epiphany, to start their program two weeks later. I had already met with them several months before and made all the arrangements. The Epiphany program was very similar to Kairos Torch. Preselected youth would again participate for three days and then Epiphany team members would commit to mentor them for a six-month period as well.

Soon the youth spread the word about these two programs, and it didn't take long before all of the other inmates wanted to be included. These programs were a huge success, especially with the gang boys. I knew that they would really benefit **if** they tried it **and** stayed committed. Once selected, I let them know up front, that attending **all** of the three-day sessions was mandatory as well as meeting with their mentors **every** Monday evening and they gave their word to do so.

Many of the inner-city youth from Cleveland learned to stop hating and started accepting the genuine love that came from the Caucasian Epiphany volunteers. They had never experienced any kind of spiritual activities before, especially with Caucasian Christians. Every day it was wonderful to witness the Holy Spirit working on their hardened hearts and eventually see them break down and allow the love that was penetrating their hearts to take command. Several of these tough guys were having a hard time holding back tears. I honestly enjoyed observing them take part in the activities; singing during the morning song service, and being involved, laughing and acting in the skits and games that were played. My Y.E.T. Team, Epiphany, and Kairos prayed that the **whole** experience would be something the youth would **always** remember and carry with them into the future. Our desire was that every lesson touched the heart of each boy in some way so that he could be saved and have a new spiritual life in Christ Jesus. I always loved seeing the before and after product.

Another unexpected blessing came after mentioning to several musicians from Kairos that I had guitars at the Institution. They got together with me later on and were willing to come in and teach the youth how to play. I informed the Social Workers and Unit Managers of this "new" opportunity. We had such a great response that some boys even had to be put on a waiting list! Every Monday night, the Kairos music instructors came in several hours before their mentoring meetings started for guitar classes. These men were now serving in two capacities back-to-back, and I thanked God for them!

Preparing ahead of their scheduled arrival time, I made sure that everything was set- up in the library; guitars, amplifiers, and seating arrangements ready to go. The Correction Officers made sure to call me when they came. Usually, I would already be up front or on my way there to greet and escort them over to our bookroom. The music program was exciting! The Recreation Director and I even became involved. We were "eager" students taking the lessons each week along with the boys and enjoyed everything being taught. These "extra" activities helped reinforce how beneficial implementing programs was to enrich the youth, broadening their minds, and giving them something to look forward to.

One of our own classroom teachers heard about the lessons from a youth already participating. She told me that her husband also played guitar and wouldn't mind giving lessons. So, I was able to enroll him in our next volunteer training class and put him to work as soon as possible. Youth were assigned to him for instruction and sometime later, other volunteers joined us and taught harmonica and drum lessons as well.

I will praise thee, O LORD,
with my whole heart;...
-Psalm 9:1

Fund Raising Projects

"What love is this!"

I was especially happy to see that all of our music classes
were being successful. For back in 2006, the Calvary
Lutheran Church in Chillicothe, Ohio had heard about
our need for volunteers and assistance to finance whatever
projects we were doing at the time. Their Choir Leader, Mrs.
Kn., called the institution. She was concerned about our most
pressing needs and offered to help. The Administrative Deputy, my supervisor, informed me that she would be calling
me soon. I did hear from her directly and we talked exten-
sively about how her group could be of service to us. Not long
afterwards, she contacted me again with great news! God had
answered her group's prayers and now she readily shared
their fantastic idea with me.

On Saturday, April 1, 2006, at 7 p.m., they held a fund-rais-
ing concert entitled "For the Love of the Son." The community
came together in full force and rallied to help us.

They had over nineteen community churches made up of a
sixty-six-member choir participate. The event turned out better than we had hoped for with more than four hundred thir-
ty-seven people in attendance and over two thousand dollars
raised to buy needed youth Bibles. How well I remember that
awe-inspiring event!

Now, I was in need again. I wanted instruments for these young men. I knew that everybody didn't play sports so I thought how great it would be if we had musical instruments available for them. Again, a call came from Mrs. Kn. right on time. She and her assistant, K., wanted to have another concert to supply our boys with additional items that would benefit them the most.

Another concert was thoughtfully planned, and the date set for April 20, 2009. It was called "Praise of the Son." Approximately fifty choir members from twenty various community churches came this time to perform and their church members once again faithfully supported the event. The concert raised over twenty-five hundred dollars that afternoon. The Y.E.T. Team and I were present along with our Superintendent.

The singing was angelic and the Holy Spirit's presence filled the sanctuary. I was asked to bring my team up front. There, waiting for us, were two brand new electric guitars! They had been graciously donated by the local music store, and lovingly presented right then, contributing to our cause. The Superintendent, Y.E.T. Team, and I were elated and very grateful for what this Church community had done for us. I will **never** forget the genuine Christian love that the Calvary Lutheran Christian Church showed us! We truly had a wonderful, spiritual time visiting their Church that afternoon.

Later on, the following month, I was able to purchase a complete set of drums from the local music store; several saxophones, harmonicas, and three acoustic guitars. All of this was an answer to prayer. So, **have faith** and **believe** that God can and will bless you with whatever your need is! I did not have a budget or could not usually get what I needed from the Administration for my Religious Department. But I always knew that God would hear me and answer my prayers.

I always taught the youth that "Prayer is the key in the hand of faith that unlocks Heaven's storehouse." (Ellen G. White, Steps to Christ, pp. 94) God sent volunteers that were faithful and obedient and who were willing to serve and supply us with what we were in need of each and every time. The youth at the facility began to feel better about themselves and had something other than a dark room of incarceration and doom. They had something to look forward to that they loved and wanted to learn about.

The Correction Officers were very polite to the music volunteer instructors and especially receptive to their program. They were happy to bring the boys over whenever I called because it proved to be a positive "win-win" situation for the youth and themselves. The youth got to enjoy the classes and the C.O.'s got to see marked changes in the young men's attitudes making their jobs easier. I always checked to see that a current music schedule was posted on each Unit and personally remind the "C.O.'s" myself about these activities so that no mix-ups would occur with group and practice times. Besides handling all preliminaries, I made sure that arrangements were in place for lessons to continue in the event of my absence. The majority of the time, however, I was there in the group participating too because for me, it was both rewarding and fun.

Blessed be the Lord, who daily loadeth us with benefits, even the God of our salvation...
-Psalm 68:19

24

Retirement

...things did not remain the way I had hoped.

I retired in the Spring of 2010 on May 1st. Before I left, however, I wrote out a complete schedule for each week and month for all of my programs. The names of volunteers, days and times for specific houses involved, and a list of participants was included. I was attempting to make the transition easier for the next Chaplain to carry on with the programs already successful, so that everything would **not** end. Unfortunately, things did not remain the way I had hoped.

The female Chaplain after me only needed one year to retire. So, she was in and out of our facility very quickly. Her term proved not an adequate amount of time to establish a viable relationship with the boys, staff, or volunteers and was over at the end of 2011. The next Chaplain who came to replace her choose not to stay long either. His previous assigned institution, **ORV**, had been closer to home for him and now closed in 2011 as well. His transfer to us began immediately in January 2012. However, after considering the added stress to be placed on his family and additional travel time required from southern Ohio to **Cir** every day, he accepted a State Parole Officer position in his locale instead.

Meanwhile, waiting for the Chaplain's replacement, the youth and volunteers were adversely affected. Reliable sources shared with me how the boys hadn't received any spiritual guidance or Church services in months and were beginning to get out of hand. At the same time, the Institution steadily received "new" youth belonging to one gang or another. Such conditions did not lend themselves to maintaining any type of peaceful atmosphere and no one was communicating with the volunteers. Naturally, they stopped coming; especially when the Operations Administrator would not allow them on Units. This situation was unfortunate because before my leaving officially, over one hundred twenty-five "active" volunteers were coming in throughout the month. They were steadily conducting mentoring, tutoring, Bible Studies, and sporting activities for me. Besides that, our Y.E.T. Team, without having proper leadership anymore, fell by the wayside too since no one really stepped up to lead out.

I recall getting an email asking me to come in on Sunday, September 11, 2011, from one of my former volunteers who was still there. She had organized a team to pray for the Staff and Institution. I agreed to go and saw one male Correctional Officer that told me, "Chap, it has never, ever been this bad. I hate coming to work." He was someone who **never** complained and one of the best C.O.s that I had worked with! As I walked through the lobby, others, both male and female, stopped me who felt the same way.

They were all depressed and fearful expressing how dire the atmosphere was presently pervading on grounds. I was sorry to hear things had deteriorated to this degree.

Many of them asked me if I was coming back because of the dilemma. They said that there was no Church services or prayer for the youth and the Holy Spirit of joy and peace was gone again. "We all dread being at this place." was their cry.

With all of these positive components on hold or completely undone for so long, the youth found other ways to exert their energy. I was told on October 27, 2011, that a riot started on grounds. Youth coming from the Gym and another Unit coming from the cafeteria broke ranks and began fighting in the middle of the yard. Staff were injured and it took everyone there, meaning **all** Staff, to try to get them to stop! This incident became so bad that S.W.A.T. was called in and had to pepper spray the boys to get things back under control. All youth involved were then placed on lock down.

After my departure in May of 2010, one young man was selected to become the next Superintendent. I knew him from my early years. We had worked together briefly when I was the Chaplain at the Freedom Center. Some staff called me, however, to report that he was unfortunately not equipped to handle the position and as a result only lasted six months. So, now, once again, **another** person was called in to be the Superintendent but this time someone who had had much more experience.

One morning in June of 2012, I got a call from Mr. E., the current Superintendent. I was very surprised to hear from him. He asked me if I would consider coming back to serve as Chaplain. I felt his concern and need for help. I told him that I was not really interested but would pray about it and discuss the situation over with my wife and family first. In the meantime, Mr. E. told the Staff that I **was** coming back before I had given him my answer! Maybe he did it to give them some type of hope because things were so bad. Contacting him soon afterwards, I told Mr. E. that I would return under certain conditions. Namely, being able to serve the way I was accustomed to being my main priority because things were totally changed from when I was there. With God's guidance, I knew reestablishing Church services and a "trust" relationship with the boys, recalling volunteers, and reestablishing effective programs would be possible while helping create a better working atmosphere and boosting staff morale once again. He told me "No problem" and that we could work all these things out.

Unfortunately, politics got involved and Central Office **told** the Superintendent that he had to offer someone transferring from the adult prison system the position **before** an "outside" person could apply. I was very surprised to hear this news. What I eventually realized though was that all the main Central Office "elect" were gone now and those who replaced them didn't know me personally. They probably only **heard** about me.

Yet, I felt that even with this limited knowledge, it should have been enough to warrant rehiring me if they really wanted to get the Institution back in order.

Many times, I was invited to attend special events held on grounds by the Recreation Director. He would always notify me about their up-coming occasions, especially those sports related. Now, he had asked me to attend a football game between the youth and the Columbus Police Professional Football Team. It took place one Sunday afternoon at about 1 p.m. The Superintendent along with most of the Staff, who didn't usually work on Sundays, were there. They barbecued hamburgers and hot dogs and had certain pre-selected units out to watch the game. I met the Coach of the Columbus team, after he had finished praying with them, at the end of a great game. His team had won by two touchdowns. I introduced myself and was invited to the library for a special workshop and book presentation being led by one of the players. He was a Columbus native who had played football for Ohio State and the NFL. Everyone, including myself, received an autographed copy of his book. I really enjoyed being there.

Afterwards, while walking down the school hallway, one of my former volunteers saw me and was elated that I was there. She was getting ready to start Church Services, in one of the classrooms, and wanted me to conduct it. I thanked her but refused because the Chaplain was not there that day. I did stay though and attended the Service. It was nice because she had with her a "new" volunteer, a student from the college nearby, who brought the message. She still involved me in the Service, however, by giving closing prayer.

When I was leaving, after I had been there about four hours or so, I ran into one of the Social Workers who was in the parking lot getting out of her car. She was happy to see me and I felt the same way. After we finished greeting one another, she began telling me how bad things had gotten. She recalled how the State Highway Patrol's S.W.A.T. Team was called to the facility recently because four Black males had locked themselves into a twelve by ten-foot game room with probably nothing in there to harm themselves or anyone else. It has thick glass full length windows that you can see every-one inside. The four males said that they were not coming out until their demands were met which consisted of having four pizzas and a young woman.

Now, in my mind, it wouldn't take an entire S.W.A.T. Team to defuse the situation. We were trained to use verbal skills along with intelligence to handle things of that nature. I was also told by this person and others about the same situation and how it was not necessary for the S.W.A.T. Team to be called in. The Superintendent did not make this decision, but it was however mandated from downtown's Central Office by individuals who usually had never worked a Unit and unfa-miliar with DYS procedures. S.W.A.T. came in, broke the door down, and dragged the boys across the carpet while having their guns drawn and ready to shoot. I felt that this was totally unnecessary and could have easily turned into an uglier mess. Thank God that it didn't!

And now, Lord,...my hope is in thee.
-Psalm 39:7

25

Putting My Faith
& Trust in God

*"They do not know **ME**. Teach them who **I** am."*

I can remember when I first became the "new" Chaplain. The Interim Superintendent, who I had never met until then, called me to his office. He presented me with a gold coin that said, "Believe and Succeed." These were sentiments that I had always felt convicted of and valued. My confidence was in knowing that I had a solid educational background behind me and a memorable "on the job" experience with the previous, recently retired Chaplain. Both qualifiers had prepared me to serve. In addition, my "active" participation as a local Elder, for seven years, at my home Church along with being employed as a Drug Counselor were beneficial as well. Now, I knew that I was ready to serve as "the" full-time Chaplain for the Department of Youth Services because I was already serving as a "Contract" Chaplain for them starting in 1993 at the Freedom Center working with the boys and girls there. Most importantly though, is the fact that I had faith in **God** knowing that **He** called me to the ministry!

There is a big difference between a Pastor serving at a Church and a Seventh-day Adventist Chaplain serving at a prison facility. First of all, the Church Pastor usually starts with a congregation. Then, he or she builds from there, learning his member's needs, problems, strengths, talents, family members, and so forth. It is very common for him to have a Choir, Deacons, Deaconess, Church Board, and Elders who work with him or her to build up the household of faith.

He, along with his Treasurers and Assistants, help keep the finances in order. His Elders help with Prayer Meeting, member visitation, hospital visits, and funeral services. Everybody comes together under the leadership of the Pastor who generally holds monthly meetings to communicate with these groups so everyone will be aware of what's going on in the Church. Then, there is your Personal Ministry Director, Community Services Director, Single Ministry Leader, Senior Citizens Leader, and your Disability Director just to name a few other departments that help the Pastor with Church ministries for the members and community. This type of cooperation is great when everyone is doing his or her part for the Church.

Now, serving as a Chaplain, however, requires and includes additional tasks and duties. So many people do not know what a "Chaplain" even means let alone what he does! Just like the Pastor of the Church, a Chaplain preaches, teaches, counsels, and leads his members. He also prays for them and their families and is responsible for spiritual leadership. The Chaplain does all this and more.

He is the "Pastor" at the facility for the Staff **and** the youth. For instance, I was responsible for handling **all** religious affairs dealing with inmates from giving religious assessments to helping serve them better in their respective faiths. Counseling youth with specific needs when requested, leading Bible study groups, providing Bibles and other religious materials, taking boys off grounds for funerals, and making hospital visits with them to see seriously ill family members was just a part of my day. Preaching weekly Church services, holding

"Week of Prayer" meetings, and hosting other area Churches and Pastors to conduct revivals were scheduled on a regular basis. In addition, I directed baptismal classes myself and held baptisms after Church Services.

My calendar also included giving periodic workshops and scheduling volunteers to work with the young men each week. They were people from the community who I had personally met and **individually** trained prior to being assigned. This procedure was a safeguard that I felt necessary since volunteers came under my department and I would be held accountable for anything that went wrong and/or their actions.

Another one of my duties required being responsible for all Bibles and religious materials entering the institution. There was a multitude of things coming in constantly such as: items from parents, book companies, advertisements, things youth would order without permission, you name it. And it came! All kinds of contraband books and materials would end up on the Units as well, items that I did not approve or put there, namely, wiccan bibles and books, voodoo books, unauthorized bibles of scientology and more.

The question was "How were these books getting in, if I did **not** approve them?" Also, "who were the ones bringing them in?" The entire Staff knew the rules about policy and procedures because they were all in training and signed off that they had been trained **and** understood the policies. "**Contraband**" was defined as "any object that violates the Ohio Revised Code and considered a threat to the facility". Regardless of this fact, many times some Staff **still** brought things in secretly and did whatever they could to get away with it. This was a constant battle I had to fight. The majority of Correction Officers, however, did respect the rules and informed me when these items were found on their units.

The Superintendent had given me permission though to distribute and circulate positive reading materials such as: Bibles (pre-approved by me), handouts, daily devotionals, and other similar resources to encourage and be of benefit to our prison population. I provided this literature on all six units. In addition, I had a religious library, in my office, where youth could check out books by signing them out with their name, date, and assigned Unit.

Sometimes during the year, Operations would schedule an unannounced search for "contraband" on the whole grounds. Cords, ropes, shoestrings, wires, chains, cell phones, knives, fingernail files, paper clips, glass, cigarettes, matches, and lighters were among the objects to be confiscated plus others. Staff and volunteers were well aware of the complete list of unacceptable articles. All books and materials of a religious nature were boxed up and given to me. Then they were sorted and those approved were returned to their respective units.

Keeping youth engaged in positive activities was essential but in 2004, an incident occurred during a routine search. A Correction Officer found nude pictures of males and females hidden in the mattress of an inmate. After a further investigation, the youth admitted that he had bought them. He reported that pictures were being sold and passed on during school time. In about a month's time, Security (or Operations) was finally able to trace the photos back to another youth who was deemed the "leader". He was someone the other boys looked up to.

The situation did not stop there. Upon checking the young man's room, boxes of candy bars, soap, toothpaste, Honey Buns, ink pens, paper, stamps and other contraband "goodies" were discovered. He also had bags of prescription pills that he had acquired from boys who were on meds pretending to have swallowed them in front of the nurse, but instead had held them under their tongues. These powerful psychotropic medications were being passed along during the day until reaching this "leader" and as a result, many of the youth were getting high off of these medications for quite a while before any of this was even uncovered.

Then, while in Computer class, the boys somehow got the security code and hacked into the DYS system downtown changing their release dates to their advantage. It was amazing what these young people learned how to do negatively. What would happen if they put their energy into doing the right things! After the investigation, the Computer Instructor was fired having to assume responsibility for their actions. All of the school's computers were examined to see if anyone else was involved and this Teacher, a long-time employee, married, and well-respected man, was unfortunately blamed for the entire situation.

I earnestly had to pray for God to keep me aware of the infiltration of satan's strategies that he would use to get through to the vulnerable minds of these youth. Satan made things appealing to them, especially if they had been hurt, mistreated, and mentally or physically abused. They would easily want to rebel and **not** trust or listen to adults telling them to behave, don't act out and go to school and make something of yourself.

Many of the psychologists would ask me to see a youth who had problems sleeping or could not adjust with the others on a unit. I would always ask to see his file so that I could know more about him. I found a number of files to be as thick as telephone books. It was really unbelievable to read about what these boys had been through so young; a lot of tragedy, rape, and mental abuse from parents not raising them properly. They had seen fighting in the home, shootings, and killings. Some had witnessed their mothers having sex with different partners while they were in the same room, had seen their parents using and abusing drugs, and had even gotten high while partying along with their parents.

I can recall on one occasion, the psychologist asked me to see a particular youth. After first reading his file, I had him come over to my office for counseling when school had let out for the day. He was a very nice youth, that I had nicknamed "Red Carrot Top" because of his extra bright, red hair. He was noticeably respectful and mannerable for a lot of those incarcerated did not come across like that. I asked him what was his problem and he told me that he could not sleep at night. I asked him, "Why?" He said that every night a man comes and sits on his bed. So, he can't sleep. I asked him how long this had been going on and he replied that it had started when he arrived about three weeks ago. I asked him, "Did the man say anything?" and he responded, "No".

I had read about some parents going out in the woods having some sort of worship, circling around a fire chanting words and drinking blood from cats. They would have their children participating with them.

Numerous youth that came to us had had bad role models and terrible experiences in their lives before they reached fifteen. These factors certainly had a detrimental effect on their behavior and the need for professional help. Some would require years of professional counseling to help them overcome the trauma of what they had been through. Having a "normal" childhood with loving parents, caring siblings, and a safe home environment and community to grow up in unfortunately had not been theirs.

After asking "Red Carrot Top" more questions, he said how he had wanted to know about demons and had read a little about it in a book. He also stated that he had gotten into pills and smoking pot. I told him what I wanted to do and that was to visit him at the same time the man was coming to his room. I counseled Red for several weeks and I visited his room. Of course, nobody showed up. I prayed with him and read him scriptures from God's word, and I let him read it out loud. I anointed his room when he was at school and after two weeks, Red could sleep peacefully. His psychologist was happy after I gave her my report and she checked up on him in school as well as on the Unit. Every time I went to make my rounds, I would see Red, now playing cards, laughing, and at peace. He said the man on his bed never came back!

By the way, I don't believe that he made it up. Other youth had told me that they were hearing voices in their heads a lot, telling them things. Sometimes I think these things occurred because "avenues" had been opened for satan to penetrate their minds, by their using drugs, playing demonic games, alcohol use, and mental illness.

Besides the youth, several Correction Officers approached me to get my thoughts concerning strange things happening late at night on third shift. They told me about times when all the lights were out and everything was quiet, footsteps were heard. It seemed as if someone was walking around but no one was ever seen. Doors were opening and closing, even though the assigned Officer on duty wasn't doing rounds! Hearing weird sounds of someone coming down the steps yet nobody being there was disturbing as well. Five to six officers reported the same occurrences. After a while, their Unit Managers were informed and together, "we", discussed the situation.

Eventually, the Managers who were Christians, asked me to pray for their Units, Officers, and youth. They also requested for these Units to be "anointed". Willingly, I agreed, and prayed for everyone. I made a point of talking to and reassuring the staff; especially giving them the moral support they needed at the time. They became encouraged. I knew that God would hear and answer the petitions made in their behalf and drive out those evil spirits. The same ones I had to battle and constantly deal with because in prison, there is noise, tension, and arguing all the time. No peace! Satan strives non-stop to cause confusion and wreak havoc to upset youth and staff. So, every quarter, I faithfully anointed each Unit. I knew for a fact that **God** was the **only** One with the power to handle all the dangerous and evil situations that continually came up throughout the days and weeks!

When you become the Chaplain there's not any of these things in place that a Pastor has. I had **all** of those responsibilities on my own for the first three years of serving. I had to pray and go out into the community and the surrounding cities to recruit volunteers. God answered my prayers and began to send them to the facility asking for me.

In the beginning God was the "Elder" Board! I did not have any help at first. But through serving Him faithfully, God will send you what you need to succeed. Just keep trusting and praying. There is a saying that, "All Chaplains can be a Pastor, **but** not all Pastors can be a Chaplain." I really found this out to be so true. For instance, one **cannot be fearful** because if you are, the inmates smell "fear" quickly and they will take advantage of you to use you every time. You must **stand tall and be firm** especially when confronted by the inmates. Look them in the eyes and say what you mean and **mean what you say**! **Don't make promises** that **you can't keep**. They already have had many disappointments and let downs in their lives. They don't need any from us. Also, one must really **know the Bible** and **stand up for what you believe in**.

You **must not be afraid of confrontations** because God uses those instances to present truth in different circumstances, especially being a Seventh-day Adventist Chaplain. Many times, God opened the door for me to witness about the Sabbath, health laws, as well as prophecy. When **911** took place, it caused a frightening effect everywhere. I was asked by the Superintendent at the time, if I would help bring some explanation, calmness, and understanding to our facility. We had an assembly that week and he had everyone attend. All Staff were present and for fifteen minutes I spoke on sin, salvation, and the Second coming. I prayed and God gave me what to talk about, so I did. Amazingly, it brought understanding, calmness, and awareness of the times in which we live. That August, A.C.M., Adventist Chaplain Ministries, had just sent me three cases of The Great Controversy and The Desire of Ages books to distribute. The Staff and the youth were lining up at my door to get them. Bible Studies increased on the Units and Staff asked to hold prayer and studies with them at lunch times. Every following year, after we held a memorial assembly outside to remember 911.

In my experience of being a Chaplain, I have witnessed a large number of Chaplains somewhat reluctant to stand on certain issues. They even hesitate to speak up for themselves with issues that the State directives would back them up on. I was never afraid to do my job. Knowing and relying on the directives gave me confidence. I was able to proceed wholeheartedly especially when it came to youth rights or my own job responsibilities.

I always knew If God really called one and the State hired you, who can hold you back from serving Him in your job, especially with the State directives giving you the right.

But unfortunately, some were still fearful. They wanted me to make available and set up whatever I was doing for them at their institutions. When I first became the Chaplain, I asked God what is it that He wanted me to do at the facility. He said, "They, meaning the youth and even Staff, do not know **ME**."

"Teach them who I am." To me, that meant His Holy Word, The Bible, for all of my Bible Studies.

I had instructed the volunteers to teach the youth about **His** faith, love, and have concern for everyone no matter what race, color, or creed. After that, I knew that they had to see this in me just like Jesus stated to the disciples that had been with Him for over three years. "Have you been with Me all this time and you ask, Show me the Father?" I knew that He was in me, so I tried every day to let them see Him through my serving Him. When others see Christ in you, the Holy Spirit does everything else. Friendship, respect, love, and understanding follows in all that you do.

What made my ministry successful was that I **always put prayer first**. In my personal prayers, I prayed for wisdom and discernment. Every day you're faced with decisions and constantly being asked for by youth as well as Staff. This is because they all needed personal family counseling. I prayed for health and strength so I would be able to do my job properly. I covered the grounds every day visiting the whole facility, making sure things and people were okay. This exchange was so important because it doesn't take much for those incarcerated to lose their tempers. So, I always wanted to be seen and help make a pleasant atmosphere for them, even though they were imprisoned.

Believe it or not, a smile or a pat on the back goes a long way when humans are locked up. My schedule was conveniently posted on the wall in my office and followed faithfully by me Sunday through Thursday. When I went to the Units, I always looked to see who was in "lock-up" (meaning a youth who was in trouble on his Unit and had to be put in isolation for some time). Then, I would tell the Correction Officers of my plans to visit that particular youth and find out directly from him what he was in for. Usually, the juvenile was very glad to know that he would now have someone to talk to, especially if the visit was with the Chaplain. These were vital times for me to instruct, encourage, and help those youth get on the right path, and always proved to be very positive.

Trust in him at all times;...pour out your heart
before him: God is a refuge for us...
-Psalm 62:8

26

No Help, Know Help, Making a Difference

"Invest!" tho' blessed..."

In the juvenile system, I was very shocked, or should I say surprised, when I discovered that after a youth was released, the community at-large nor institutions had any post-prison programs in place for him. There were no organizations to help with positive reentry into society. Collaborations for this type of interaction between the prison system and groups outside the prison walls was non-existent. Instead, Correction Officers often informed me how they would take boys to the bus station and drop them off, even though these young men had at least one "parent," to go home to.

In many situations, however, there were families who did **not** want his or her son to return because their cases involved sexual offenses. Instead, these fathers and or mothers would intentionally move; not wanting the young person to know exactly where they were. I spoke to several parents who did not even trust their loved ones at all anymore. This was primarily due to the fact that numerous times the victim had been a family member. These special cases should be addressed and dealt with for the victims as well as for the released youth. What happens to these young men who enter the community?

Usually a disappointing dilemma, since most haven't finished high school, have no technical training or skills, and their felonies prevent them from going into the Armed Forces.

Correction Officers would also let released youth out at a homeless shelter or Friends of the Homeless facility with only the clothes on their backs, no money, no identification; **only** themselves! For those who were sex offenders, registering and reporting in the area where they lived was expected, but many did not do this. Where do they go? What were they doing in the communities? Each youth would be assigned a Probation Officer who probably had a "boat load" of cases and couldn't always keep track of his whereabouts. Who's held responsible for their actions? The majority of these guys are on meds, provided by the State while incarcerated, but now, they are without food, shelter, **and** medication! These factors create a disaster just waiting to happen!

The only in-house program, that I was aware of, was a mandatory "Victim Awareness" class lasting eight weeks for all sex offenders. Various Social Workers taught the class and would always ask me to attend so I could answer any questions dealing with the Bible and forgiveness. However, not having actual after-release community support services was a real problem and made it easier to see how they could be led astray again **just** to survive. If unable to get a job, due to their felony records and no high school diploma, resorting to theft and other crimes becomes their choice. Eventually, if these young men are not killed by rival gangs, they end up returning to prison, adult prison now. What do you do with them then? What kind of programs are available to help them educationally? The college ones that were in place got cut!

In my opinion, instead of using taxpayer money to "incarcerate" youth, "invest" in them! It makes more sense to have educational systems set up **in** prison so guys that have seen the error of their ways **can** become accomplished and trained. Then, when finally released, they will have a "good" education or job skills enabling them to have a fair chance in becoming productive citizens.

In spite of any inadequacies, we were still blessed with our Christian volunteers from the surrounding community. To my knowledge, **they** were providing the only programs involved with the juvenile prison system. These were faith-based and presented by dedicated, committed individuals. Countless hours were spent every week on Bible Study, workshops, Christmas programs, plays, outdoor Gospel-fests, and discipleship, evangelistic meetings to help prepare those incarcerated for a successful future. I feel that enough cannot be said about how valuable volunteers are. They drive for miles when they get off work, sacrifice spending time with their own family to come, and use their own money on gas to see the inmates.

I can recall, my **second year**, in fact, that I requested funds to buy certificates for **my** volunteers. The Administrator, at the time, laughed at the very idea. I was told "no!" and "Make them one and make some copies to give to the rest of them." I did not think it was funny and decided from then on to let **every** volunteer know just how much they were appreciated and welcome. I had personally trained each one and purposely escorted them around; making sure to introduce them to Staff and youth alike. Every time I saw a volunteer was an opportunity for me to tell him or her again how special they were **and** how happy **I** was that God had sent them to help me! All through the years, I was determined to teach the Correction Officers **and** the Administration how important and valuable volunteers are.

Let thy mercy O LORD, be upon us,
according as we hope in thee.
-Psalm 33:22

27

T.I.C.O. Riots - 1996

"infiltrating young minds..."

One day I remember going into the Superintendent's office. All of his Deputies were there as well as his replacement. He was being transferred soon to another facility and they were all talking about something, but nothing very serious, when I walked in. I said, "Excuse me. I just wanted to stop by and offer the Superintendent a word of prayer". The Superintendent, however, declined and said, "Thank you but no thanks." Then, they began to laugh when I was leaving, mostly at him though, and not at me. In due time, however, he would realize **just** how important **and** needed that refused prayer was!

It was about three months later when his "new" facility had one of the worst riots in the entire Ohio juvenile system. This incident occurred the summer of 1996. I was home, getting ready to eat dinner, when I sat down and turned on the evening news. They were showing "live" coverage of the Riot Squad pulling up to T.I.C.O. I saw about six vans and the S.W.A.T. Team in full riot gear. They had shields, guns, and their rifles out as they ran into the building.

I was shocked seeing this happening right in front of me. Being genuinely concerned about everyone's safety, I went into another room and started praying asking God to intervene.

I already knew about problems at this prison because their Chaplain had shared his concerns with the nine other Correctional Chaplains during our monthly meetings. At those times, we would all pray for our facilities and share what we were struggling with there.

The Chaplain at T.I.C.O. had informed us that for some time he was having problems with the volunteer Muslim Imam. He stated that youth were recruiting other youth to become Muslims because of him and how this Instructor was also teaching them to disregard prison rules. For example, he was encouraging the boys to demand various things for themselves, and **if** not received right away, take action themselves! As a result, the youth wanted to have everything their way; with their food, times to meet with the Imam, and designated visitors. These were only a few of their demands and changes they mandated to be made.

I, personally, had an interest in what happened at T.I.C.O. because it was where I first started working back in 1990. The Superintendent that was called back there was the one who had originally hired me! The Chaplain from T.I.C.O. would consistently ask us, his fellow clergymen, for prayer and always kept us up to date on happenings at his institution. We informed him that he should contact Central Office and let them know the situation. He told us that he **had** already reported this dilemma to them constantly **but** to no avail. Nothing was ever done.

Even though I was busy at my own job, I tried to counsel him on how to handle this particular Muslim volunteer. For you see, earlier that spring, this **same** young man, about in his late twenties, had come to Circleville! He hadn't called me or made an appointment. He just came! Then, I got a call to come up front. I brought him in the exact way I would do any new person wanting to volunteer and help serve our youth.

He stated that he was an Imam Muslim minister and wanted to "minister" giving studies to my youth. I informed him that I did **not** have any Muslim youth at the time but when I did, I would gladly call him so that afterwards he could go through the proper volunteer training.

I made it clear to him, however, that he was to "minister" **only** to Muslim youth and **not** try to take my place as the sole religious leader. Instruction for boys of varying faiths was already being provided. Case in point: when I had a Jewish youth, which was very rare, he was **not** to see an Imam. I had his Rabbi come in to serve him. The same procedure was provided for a Catholic or Seventh-day Adventist youth. They would see a Minister from their **own** respective faith with permission from their parents.

What happened at T.I.C.O. was very tragic and should **never** have happened! Looking back, I was told by several of their Staff that these religious youth meetings held by the Imam grew rapidly. Everyone was requesting to take part and convert to Islam. Somehow, on that terrifying evening, the young men overran an area, took keys from Officers, and ran into classrooms brutally injuring several female teachers. One teacher was even stabbed in the face with a pencil!

A Recreation employee, who was on duty, said that he had just locked the gate in time as the rioting youth were running to get to the gym **and** to the Chaplain's office. These angry boys wanted to hurt the Chaplain because he had said that only a certain number of them were allowed to attend the Muslim meetings. I was also told how they were totally out of control, smashing everything in sight, yelling, and cursing like madmen. **If** it hadn't been for that particular Recreation employee, the gate would have been torn down as well. His action helped to keep them back until help arrived. When it was all over that evening, many Staff had to be taken to the hospital; several with broken bones, lacerations, and other severe injuries.

Months passed. The damaging effects and impact of this unfortunate incident were still evident. Central Office **should** have intervened and listened to the Chaplain when he told them that he needed help and things were getting out of hand. Instead, they turned a deaf ear and all of the unnecessary trouble that was caused could have been avoided! Also, the Imam should have been monitored and **not** allowed to teach the youth untruths filling their minds with "hateful" messages. Nothing uplifting or essential about self-discipline, respect, loving your neighbor, and having integrity was taught but only hate and violence, which fueled those young men to turn out. As for me, I stood strong and did **not** allow that type of negativity to happen "on my watch", at my facility, even though some tried.

This is why I continued to push for positive programming because programming, I found, to be of true value when dealing with incarcerated youth. Even though education, of course, would prove to be first in importance, youth tend to be very responsive to organized activities. For example, the Recreation Department provided indoor activities in the winter months such as basketball, dodgeball, volleyball, and board games twice a day for each Unit. Then, in the spring and summer, basketball, softball, track, and other sporting events took place. Being outdoors, running, laughing, walking, talking to friends, listening to music, breathing fresh air is good for the body, mind, and spirit **and** especially for those locked up! Most of the time, these activities helped relieve the stress and anxiety of prison life.

Having recreational activities though was only one valuable and needed component for working with young people. In my opinion, addressing their spiritual needs is just as vital. Here are young men who are in their "growing" stages, both mentally and physically with plenty of testosterone and energy to spare. **All** three areas: mind, body, **and** spirit need to be nurtured otherwise "we", the adults serving them, do them a disservice because when youth are not properly trained, they will resort to "creations" of their own to fill the void.

The "virus" of gangs has penetrated our facilities from the cities to the state prisons around the United States. What is essential though is to start a rapport with these boys. Being truthful and real goes a long way. Believe me, they will know **if** you're genuine, honest, or fake. Once they realize that you care, they **will** listen to you! Then, the same ones will begin to open up and trust you with their inner most feelings about their lives, how they sincerely feel, and what they're actually going through. That's why each day they must put on a "tough" face and be strong to survive the atmosphere they're in; and the reason I **always** let them know that I was available anytime they needed me.

To help deal with the gang life crisis, special guests were invited to speak at entire population assemblies. Derrick Russell, the leader of the Short North Posse Gang, accepted my invitation and came. His gang had become infamous in causing havoc in Columbus, Ohio neighborhoods. Derrick was released from prison after serving ten years. He had learned his lesson of wrongdoing and recently written a book called Listen Good Youth. Since becoming a Christian and giving his life over to the Lord, he now coaches young people in football. His goal today is dedicating his life, talking to youth about his mistakes, and helping deter them from making the same bad choices. Anytime I would call him, he did not hesitate to come in and willingly spoke to our boys on several occasions. Derrick would also go with me to individual Units and talk to those who were in "lock-up" for inappropriate behavior.

Seeing his powerful impact on our youth, I advised other interested Chaplains and Superintendents to arrange for him to relate his life story at their institutions as well.

Another invited guest was Carl Upchurch, who had been personally involved with gangs and gang life. He was an ex-con and gang member who became a great activist for peace that inspired a television movie and book entitled <u>Convicted In The Womb</u>.

After hearing his outstanding, testimonial stories, selective workshops, that I had prearranged, were held for the most aggressive young men followed by question-and-answer sessions. We were all genuinely impressed with his life stories and how he matured, resulting in turning his life around. I saw his movie and had him autograph his book for me. Several copies were put in the library for the boys to read at their convenience as well.

28

Volunteers & Rule Infractions

"...know the directives, like you know your Bible!"
Observe principles and rules first.

— Old-timer employee

T here were many hindrances on my job that made it very complicated at times. A certain number of staff would try to perform my job duties by counseling youth and giving them unauthorized Bible studies. These areas were my responsibility and yet, particular teachers or Correction Officers would still do it; not expecting me to find out or didn't care if they got caught. I always went by the book, doing my job according to the State of Ohio directives. One "old timer" employee even advised me to "know the directives, like you know your Bible"! So, I studied them and knew them well. I treated each youth like he was my own son. I spent time with the boys, laughing, praying, mentoring, and counseling them too. My hope was that they would realize their mistakes and strive to become better people making something of their lives.

I respected all the religions that these young men came under. However, problems began surfacing when a few **Muslims** wanted to **proselytize** and recruit members in 1996. Someone of that persuasion realized that the youth would be a great investment. We had one female teacher, who had for four years, consistently given youth studies from the Quran without permission during her lunch breaks. These lessons were done secretly in her classroom because no religious materials were to be brought to the job without my authorization. However, she was sneaking these things in unofficially and always trying to undermine what I was teaching to those who were coming to Chapel every week. Her actions were definitely against Department of Youth Services policies.

I knew the rules and stood my ground on this infraction, even when my supervisor was being persuaded and pleading with me to allow it, but I did not. I simply informed him that the State of Ohio hired me to be the religious leader at the facility and that the parents trusted me to help care for their children. Then, I asked him, if **his** daughter were in here, would he like it if she became a Muslim while incarcerated? Because ninety-nine per cent of the youth that came in were under the umbrella of Christianity, services were designed accordingly. Plus, I had over one hundred twenty-five volunteers, at the time, with one hundred twenty-three Christian and two Muslim. **All** denominations had representation for their respective faiths to come in and service their youth. Not even I could proselytize in accordance with the rules and never allowed their pressure to get me to compromise on this issue.

When I reported this information to the school Principal, he kept stalling at first until I gave him written statements from the boys themselves. Then, he started his own investigation and met with this teacher several times. As a result, she also met with me and expressed her desire to become a volunteer, not really for herself only, but for her husband and several other Muslim men. I did not have a problem with this request. So, I had them complete the paperwork and personally conducted their training; the same was given to all volunteers. After training was completed, starting dates were set up for them to come in but **only** see youth who were already Muslim. I definitely went over **all** the rules. Everyone understood and agreed to adhere to them. Then they chose to meet the boys on Saturday mornings from nine to eleven a.m.

Now, my regular days off were Friday and Saturday. A month went by, and I was duly notified by a Correction Officer how the female teacher deliberately was having **whole** Units coming over to her husband's group! She had asked me if she could be with her husband and bring in an Imam for the Muslim boys to hear. However, she began baking and cooking food to entice **non**-Muslim youth to become a part of the group as well. Her recruitment plan was blocked though because the next week I came in on a Saturday, unexpectedly, while they were meeting. I graciously asked to talk to her and her husband. They knew the rules. Right then and there, I stopped her from breaking them because I had evidence on paper. Attempting to convert, not only, my institution but **all** of the other DYS facilities was their main goal and assignment according to a Pastoral Conference I had attended. One of the Muslim men coming in for studies with the two Muslim youth also verified their intent.

After this incident, they went on meeting with just the two Muslim boys for several more Saturdays, but eventually saw that they could **not** do any recruiting. The teacher continued trying to give studies during her lunch break, but it was harder to do now because she was being watched. However, determined to get her quota of recruits, she then started "using" boys by giving them treats and having them fill out request forms to become Muslims. The principal was still investigating and evaluating her movements.

Some youth told him how they had been approached by her "recruiting" efforts which deliberately broke the State's directives. This teacher consistently refused to stop, got written up for contacting youth from her classes even after they were released from D.Y.S. and so she eventually quit!

Many times, activities arose that I had to teach the Correction Officers about being honest and how to handle different situations professionally. As previously stated, I interviewed and trained **all** of my volunteers before assigning them to a Unit. They would be provided with a detailed schedule denoting their arrival times as well as inform them about where, when, and exactly how many youth would be attending their meetings. I also made sure that we were all on the same page; meaning the same subject, whether it was faith, love, forgiveness, salvation or other topics that we were teaching concurrently.

One particular Sabbath, my "off" day, as I was preparing to go to Church, I told my wife that I felt the need to go to the job first. I had the feeling that something was just not right. Arriving at my office, I found my color television was missing. I kept it locked up after discovering that Correction Officers would sometimes get it, without proper authorization, and show illicit movies to the boys. In addition, I had already arranged for each Unit to have their own "new" color television. Unfortunately, they were not taken care of and now broken or taken away because of misuse.

However, getting my T.V. out of my office meant that someone up front had given permission to pull my personal work keys. Now three people were at fault here because I had previously reported and documented how my office was being opened and my television missing on several other occasions. I looked into the middle door area designated for youth and volunteers. There was my **"new"** volunteer, a Caucasian female, who I had explicitly told what I wanted her to teach starting off, with my T.V. out! She was showing the youth what **she** wanted them to see, nothing at all what the other volunteers were teaching. I opened the door to her surprise. You should have seen her face when she saw me! The youth knew that this was not the way things were done here.

I left and called the Deputy Administrator on duty. I explained that I needed him to come over to this volunteer youth school meeting area immediately. When he arrived, I politely ended the movie and sent the youth back to their respective Houses. Then, the "new" volunteer, Deputy, and myself went into my office. I repeated the volunteer rules to her and what was expected. The Deputy saw that she did not follow the rules. I accepted her apology and then asked her if she wanted to continue being a volunteer. She said, "Yes," but never returned.

Every person in this story was Caucasian but one. Should that have made a difference? No! But it did. The fact that there are those who simply refuse, or half-way listen to someone in charge who is African American is a reality. I ran into these types of situations on more than one occasion. The "new" volunteer had been recommended by another volunteer who knew her from church. Later on, the regular volunteer told me that the "new" person was one that wouldn't listen to their Pastor and wanted to do things her way all the time. Her outlook was one of willful disregard for explicit directions given to her.

I confronted the Control Officer who was at fault because the only way one could get keys was by having a personal, assigned chip **or** by going to the Deputy for permission. I let them both know that I knew the procedure and consequences **and** had the authority to have them written up **if** I reported it. My warning to them was, "Don't let it happen again." The next person was the Officer who opened up the door and got my T.V. out for this volunteer because "she" was an attractive female of the same race! **My position and authority didn't mean anything!!**

I stood on God's principles because I knew that God wanted me to do **His will** and listen to Him. I remembered my first sermon preached there had been "too" soft and was instructed by God to speak with more fervor. I called the boys back and preached again. This time though, much more fervently, as God had wanted me to do in the first place. The Holy Spirit's presence could be felt, and afterward, I was **determined to follow** God's instructions implicitly.

So, I gave the Officer an example of a soldier and what it means to fight along with him. He's trained to **observe principles and rules first** for duty to his countrymen and fellow officers because they are his safeguards. I explained how "fighting" **together** as a team is essential because it reflects the camaraderie or disconnect of the entire group. Teamwork counts! I made him more aware of how I was responsible for all religious activities that took place on the grounds. Therefore, **if** something happened to any youth or adult that wasn't right, then, I was the one that it came back on because of his wrong decision. Do your job means just that! Doing one's part honestly and professionally, otherwise, it comes back on everyone, me, him, and the whole institution!

On another occasion in 1999, I had scheduled a particular volunteer to one of the Houses. She was to give Bible Studies to the youth in the middle section between the two Units where we held "groups" for such services. However, I had been getting some complaints from several Correction Officers telling me how she would blast her boom box when leaving the grounds as loudly as she could and shout out things as if casting out demons or something. So, as a precaution, I decided to stay over one evening on her assigned day to come in. I wanted to check for myself to see if there really was a problem and observe her group initially before talking to her.

I went to the Unit and looked through the hallway door. At first, I heard all kinds of loud noises -- shouting, hooting, and moaning. I couldn't believe what I saw either!

This woman was up on the sink with the faucet running and had several cups of water in her hands. She was throwing the water onto all twenty to thirty boys while speaking in tongues, calling herself "baptizing" them. I opened the door.

When the youth saw me, they knew that it was wrong, and somebody was in trouble. They scattered quickly and headed for their respective units. I opened the doors for them, and they went in without saying a word. The noise stopped. The volunteer cut off her boom box and jumped off the sink. I was very upset! She had broken the rules and totally disrespected me. After informing her that she could not have her own private congregation at my facility, she gradually quit coming. Several years passed before this former volunteer tried to return. This time, however, I was advised by the Administrative Superintendent not to let her come back.

In my distress I cried unto the LORD,
and he heard me.
-Psalm 120:1

29

Assaults

brutality encountered... I kept my composure and remained calm even though my mind was not expecting to see what I saw.

Working Alone

B ack in 1998, a female Correction Officer working the third shift, was attacked by two youth who had planned an escape. They had been observing her for several nights and knew she was working alone. According to prison safety guidelines and rules, however, this C.O. should **not** have been by herself with a "full" Unit of boys at any time. While on duty, she let one of these boys out to use the restroom. He caught her off guard, grabbed her walkie-talkie, and beat her until she was unconscious. Then, he released his partner. Their escape attempt was just that, "an attempt"! They were soon caught because they ran out the front door, went around to the back of the Housing Unit, climbed up on the roof, and were eventually seen.

When I arrived the next morning, I was told to see the Superintendent. He informed me what had happened and asked if I would go to the hospital and check on our Staff member. I went immediately. When I got to her room, I walked slowly to her bed. Looking at her face, I thought that I had gone into the wrong room until I saw her son and daughter sitting in the corner! Her face was terribly swollen, all black and blue. It was a very hard situation to deal with. Nevertheless, I kept my composure and remained calm even though my mind was not expecting to see what I saw. I took her hand and told her who I was. Then, I began to pray softly to God for her recovery. She was on leave for over a year.

I did not want her to return and was very upset when I saw her back on the job. I was happy though to see her walking, talking, and smiling again. We spoke, and she told me how happy it had made her feel that I came to see her. She also mentioned overhearing everything I said in the prayer and how it gave her hope and comfort while I held her hand. After thanking me, I gave her a big hug. The following day, she was gone. I found out that being on the job and around the youth once more just brought back "too" many bad memories and reminders of that terrible night! I just prayed that the State took care of her bills and disability properly.

Mr. K. - "Beat Down"

Another incident that occurred in 1998 involved Correction Officer Mr. K. He had been a very good officer for years but after some time, he seemed to change. Maybe the stress of the job or personal problems at home, like many other employees who brought their family problems to the workplace, affected him. However, one situation was brought to my attention by another Officer. Mr. K. had a scuffle with a youth who wouldn't listen to his orders and challenged him in front of the entire Unit of about thirty-two other boys. He may have roughed up the boy while putting him back in his cell along with saying some verbally abusive words. His actions probably made the young man look bad in front of his peers. The two of them more than likely began threatening one another as well because the young people would always challenge Officers believing that they could beat them in a real one-on-one encounter.

Later that summer, this guy was released and, at the time, forgotten about by the Officer. Mr. K. was now on vacation, riding around on his way home when he stopped to get gas. He parked at the pump and went in. Several young men were just hanging outside the store talking. Low and behold, the youth that the Officer had roughed up noticed that this was the **same** Officer from Circleville! He got on his cell phone and called his boys to come quick. They joined him and were all waiting for Mr. K. when he came out of the store.

These youth proceeded to jump on Mr. K., beating him unmercifully. They hit him over and over until he hit the ground. Then, about six of them began kicking him until he passed out. If it were not for a woman pumping gas at the time, he later stated, they would have killed him! Her screams made them stop and alerted the store manager to call for the police and an ambulance.

Mr. K. had to stay in the hospital for many weeks. I think it took several years before he came back to work. When I finally spoke to him, he was very different; quieter and humbler. He was not shy though when I asked him about the incident. We had really missed him during his recovery time because "his" House Three, held the worse youth! Mr. K., before this confrontation, usually had the group under control without any serious problems.

I remember while he was out how the Staff took up a collection for him and sent a get-well card signed by everybody. I know that really touched him. Unfortunately, he did not stay long when he returned. He never combated a youth who challenged him again. He learned how to use verbal, calming strategies and just let the guy run his mouth without any incidents. Due to his back and head injuries, he could not handle the daily stress and strain of the job. Physically, Mr. K. just could not do it anymore. He had to go out on disability when only in his forties. I really missed him because he was very reliable and a good C.O. role model before that one incident. His youth always came to Church in order and always very respectful at my special assemblies. I never had to discipline or write up any of his boys for unruly behavior.

That summer of 1998, I had a plaque made for Officer K. for his dedicated, outstanding service shown day in and day out. It wasn't until several years after my retirement, that I finally had the opportunity to give it to him. After receiving a call from one Circleville employee that Mr. K. had to be rushed to the ER the other evening, I went to see him. He was there, sitting in a wheelchair, along with his new fiancé and future mother-in-law. What a perfect time to present him with the plaque!

We took a picture together. He was overjoyed with happiness because, in his early years, he had been an exceptional Correction Officer and role model. One of the best! I prayed for him and his new fiancé before I left his room.

Robert - 2005

This unfortunate occurrence was the worst situation I was involved in while serving as a Chaplain. Arriving at the job, back in July 2005, I was told that a youth named Robert had gotten injured on his Unit. This was upsetting because I knew Robert. He was not one to cause trouble but very courteous and respectful instead. The week before, Robert had just given his heart to the Lord and gotten saved during Church services. My real concern for him was due to the fact that I knew how some of the other boys would try to take advantage of his kindness and now he was hurt!

The Unit Officer told me that he "appeared" to be okay and had just been "wrestling" with some guys. Later on that night, Robert went and asked the C.O. if he could come to the desk. Before the Officer could answer, however, Robert passed out on the floor. The Nurses came, called an ambulance, and rushed him to the hospital. When I got to work the next morning, I found out this additional information. I checked with the Nurses Station, and they informed me that the hospital had decided to keep him and run more routine tests.

After several days, Robert still had not returned. So, I went up front to the Superintendent's Office to get first-hand information. She told me that the situation had changed. Robert was **not** doing well. Then, I had every volunteer and Christian praying for his recovery. That same night though I got a call from the job telling me Robert had died.

The Superintendent asked to see me the next morning. She informed me that Robert's parents wanted me to hold a memorial service at the Facility for him. I made all the arrangements and scheduled the service for July 14, 2005, at 1:30 p.m. in the school gymnasium. The entire Staff and youth population were present.

Our youth Honor Guard soldiers, the "Soldiers of Christ" Youth Choir, solo by a choir member, and several boys who had written poems participated. The Superintendent spoke a few words of wisdom and the principal read the obituary. Afterwards, I stood up, went to the pulpit, and gave the opening prayer. Robert's parents were seated with me on the rostrum. When I finished, the principal handed me a note stating that the investigation by the State Patrol was over and Robert's death was in actuality a homicide!

I dare **not** tell this in my Eulogy and didn't. I was shocked but went on and spoke about Robert's character and how he had made a decision to accept Jesus Christ as his personal Saviour the week before. God truly blessed our services, and his parents were especially appreciative of how we genuinely cared and granted their wishes.

The investigation had been mandated and conducted since someone had died. The Unit's tapes were pulled by the Ohio State Patrol's Investigation Officers from the institution's Operations Station up front. Footage was reviewed from several days and revealed that some of Robert's peers were not only "wrestling" **but** "roughing" him up. Then, they discovered that his head was being slammed over and over in the doorway, using the metal door itself! Robert had, in fact, sustained a concussion, which later caused the swelling in his head leading to serious complications and tragedy. This was one of the hardest things that I had to do, knowing Robert's death was **not** from an illness or accident. I really had to pray for strength and wisdom to be able to handle these circumstances. I never knew if his parents were **ever** told the truth.

30

The Journey

Here I am (Lord); send me.

-Isaiah 6:8

I am very grateful and blessed that God called me to be a Minister and Chaplain doing service in His name. I feel that it was an honor to work for the Department of Youth Services during my entire career of over twenty years. I was able to work with the male and female populations along with their families. Working with the youth was very special and rewarding, even though it was also challenging. I had youth from all nationalities, backgrounds, cities, and states, including those who were mentally challenged, physically and or sexually abused, first-time offenders, repeat offenders, and gang bangers.

When you realize how God placed you in a position where He wanted to use the gifts and talents He gave you, helping teach and mentor others, especially the youth, that's payment enough. The young people have an opportunity to learn from their mistakes and get another chance to turn their lives around for good. Unfortunately, most of them didn't know their fathers, nor was he in their lives to help raise them. In many instances, I became "Dad" and stood in the gap.

During those vital and formative years of an adolescent, knowing someone cares and loves them **and** is genuinely concerned about their well-being is crucial. I was able to see them mature and learn because many times we had to build a foundation of "family" and love. Unfortunately, they had never experienced having such a foundation, never experienced celebrating a birthday, or never even experienced the joy of getting a birthday cake to feel special!

The newspaper generally didn't highlight our prison "success" stories. The stories of the young men who purposed in their hearts to change and better themselves were neglected or not deemed "news-worthy." When released, however, these were those who went on and graduated from Ohio State with a Master's degree, Wright State with a Bachelor's degree, and got to attend various other universities. Also, some started their businesses and even became pastors of two churches in Cleveland, Ohio. Their post-prison achievements **do** spell success **and** "worthy" to be mentioned! Many now have jobs, are married with families, and are productive citizens in their respective neighborhoods.

Several times, while out in the community, a young man would come up to me and call my name, "Chap, how are you doing?" They were always excited and couldn't wait to tell me about things they were involved in at church or at their jobs. Getting to talk with an ex-inmate personally or hear about a "success" story, even if it was only one, would feed my heart with joy because that's what serving God and my job was all about.

Through all the ups and downs, unexpected problems that arose, staff altercations, gang fights, no money for your religious department, staff and youth sicknesses and hospital visits, funerals, house blessings, counseling employees and youths' personal problems, no matter what was laid on me, I took it to the Lord in prayer. God always led me and went before and behind me, and never let me down. Every problem or situation that arose, He would always tell me what to do. I trusted Him, and **He** always worked it out!

If I could go back and choose my career all over again, I wouldn't change a thing. Through our destiny, God even shows you your past and how He was always there to put your life situations back together. The Lord brings you to where you are now **when** you put your trust in Him. All the experiences that I had in my life, good or bad, helped me to become the Christian man of God that I am today. In spite of those that were against my well-being, that may have lied or betrayed me, I was still able to persevere, by His grace, since the Bible says, "**all** things work together for those who love the Lord and are called according to His purpose." (Romans 8:28) So, I want to thank all those whom I have had the opportunity to meet; maybe we both shared and learned something from one another that benefitted our lives for the better. I know that it did for me because **God said,** "**the battle is not yours;** it belongs to **Him**"!

Appendix

Game Instructions:

"In the River on the Bank"

"In the River, On the Bank" is a fun game for entertainment. One line is placed on the ground using a long rope or a piece of tape. One side of the line will denote the "river" and the other side will represent the "bank". A facilitator is chosen to call out commands "in the river" or "on the bank" for the players to follow. All players start lining up along the side of the line which will be the "bank".

When ready, the facilitator will call out a command for the players to follow. When the facilitator calls "in the river", everyone must jump with both feet over the line to the river side. When "on the bank" is called, everyone must jump back with both feet to the bank side of the line.

The facilitator can speed up the command cadence or slow it down at their discretion. The facilitator can also repeat commands multiple times in a row to try to get players out of the game. A player is out if they get caught being "in the river" when the facilitator calls "on the bank" or vice versa. Or, a player is out if they failed to jump to the appropriate side in an adequate amount of time. If necessary, the facilitator acts as a judge to determine who should be kept in the game or who gets eliminated.

"Silly"

"Silly" is a fun game for people of all ages to play. One person is chosen at random to go into another room while the rest of the group deliberates. As the selected person is away, the group develops a dance move(s) to demonstrate for the person.

When the group is finished creating the dance, they call the person back into the room. Next, the group performs the dance for the person. The individual then has to try to mimic the dance of the group. However, the aim of the game is to try to trick the individual into thinking they aren't doing the dance correctly. The group is to not disclose to the person that they are being tricked.

After the person tries their first attempt at the dance move, the group is to explain to the person that they aren't doing the move right. The person proceeds to try again until they get it right, but they never will since the group is trying to fool them. The group can repeatedly demonstrate the dance while telling the person to dance again because the individual isn't doing it the same way as the group. This cycle continues as there is really no "right" way to do it, which is why the name of the game is called "Silly".

Memory Lane

Governor's State Employee Suggestion Award-1992

Chaplain Benton and Clark Kellog

Chaplain Benton and Lawrence Funderburke

"No Answers"

No peace can I find, to relieve stress from my mind
No cure to heal my pain, from all that's locked within
No serenity can I share, to see where I begin.
A dark cloud, fills my empty void, No answer to
my question "Why am I so annoyed"
No one there to catch my tears as they fall from
my face, how long can I endure in this hopelessness
race
Confusion storms within me, to leave me lost with no hope.
Despair and grief how ever will I cope.
Locked in a cell made by limitations, my thoughts are
barred down with no imagination.
A small cry is let out, does anyone hear a pause
of silent ruins or a drop of a tear, filled with
much sorrow. Fearing for my life will this return
tomorrow.
An endless hope wants to be set free, But a
destructive fire of rage quickly burns it out. There
fore forever leaving an eternity of doubt.
No I seem not to find a different path to take
route.
Strongest to say I never know where to begin
For the answer my soul searches for is deeply
locked within.
Theirs an Answer.

Through Darrel's Eyes

Living my life is my own prison
My heart is guarded
This is not what I envisioned

When I was small
I wanted to be brave
Run into burning buildings,
And lives I would save

At the age of nine, my innocence was taken
Oh dear God, my entire world was shaken
I felt so alone, so scared and smothered
How could he do this, the best friend of my brother?

It's so hard to forgive,
Because I did just as he did
I took the innocence of four others
How can I apologize or rectify this to their fathers' and mothers'

Lord I'm sorry for what I did
After all, they were just four innocent kids
I came here a confused boy
Now when I look in the mirror, I see a lost man

I sit here in prison
This place I regretfully call home
I dance with the thoughts of suicide
Because this pain I feel just won't subside

I'm already living in hell
I mean how would you feel
If everyday you woke up,
You were promised another day in jail?

I miss my mother, father and brother
I dwell on the fact I could have found a love in another
I miss being free and fishing on Rocky Fork Lake
But this is my life; I'm paying for my mistakes

My mind wonders about who I could have been
If only I didn't give into temptations; I have sinned
There's a hole in my heart
It's made a home here
Daily I ignore it; shrug off my loneliness and despair

2 years, 2 months and 25 days at most is all I've got
Sometimes I think I might as well stay on suicide watch
I feel so depressed and I don't know why
If I could just help myself, I wouldn't want to die

Title Unknown

Here I sit, again in jail
time here is slow, speed of a snail.
Nothing but concrete & steel
waiting for the state to make me a deal.

When they are ready to drop the dime
they will hand me down my time.
Then I will move through the system
all the while, learning new wisdom.

For this time, there's been a change in me
I have found the Lord, he is turning the key
and he too, already set me free.

About the Author

Chaplain James Benton was a Corrections Chaplain for the Department of Youth Services for twenty years in the state of Ohio when he retired in May 2010, and was also a former Drug Counselor. He has a B.A. in Theology from Oakwood University with a minor in Psychology, and a D. Div. from Agape Bible College. He currently serves as the First Elder of the Fruit of the Spirit Seventh-day Adventist Church in Columbus, OH. He is married to the former Patricia L. Groves. He has two adult children and two grandchildren. Watching sports, especially basketball is one of his favorite pastimes. He has a heart for ministry and a relentless desire to continuously serve the Lord.

www.ingramcontent.com/pod-product-compliance
Lightning Source LLC
Chambersburg PA
CBHW060911120626
46553CB00001B/288